AMERICA
AND THE
ATLANTIC
COMMUNITY

Anglo-American
Aspects, 1790-1850

AMERICA
AND THE
ATLANTIC
COMMUNITY

Anglo-American
Aspects, 1790-1850

FRANK THISTLETHWAITE

HARPER TORCHBOOKS ✦ *The Academy Library*
HARPER & ROW PUBLISHERS NEW YORK AND EVANSTON

TO JANE

Preface

THE occasion of this book was a course of public lectures given in the Fall Term of 1956 at the University of Pennsylvania as Visiting Professor of American Civilization. This Professorship, of which I had the honor to be the first holder, serves the imaginative purpose of bringing to the Graduate Department of American Civilization a European scholar in the hope that he may illuminate the cultural connections between the United States and Europe. I should like to record my admiration for the intellectual generosity which prompted the scheme and characterizes the interdisciplinary work of the Department, and to thank the University of Pennsylvania and especially its Vice-Provost, Professor Roy F. Nichols, the Chairman of the Department, Professor Robert E. Spiller, and Professor Thomas C. Cochran for what was to me a most rewarding appointment.

Because of its occasion the book was cast in lecture form and the text remains as it was delivered except for minor elaborations and the expansion into separate chapters of two sections which were unduly compressed owing to limited lecture time.

It owes something to conversations with many scholars on both sides of the Atlantic. It was especially fostered by the late John Bartlet Brebner whose work helped to focus historically ideas which grew out of wartime pre-occupations with Anglo-American relations, and whose friendship and masterly guidance were a stimulus over the years down to the last months of his life when, though ill, he gave such patient and perceptive attention to the manuscript. If Atlantic history is coming into its own, the credit must largely go to Brebner whose life, in action and study was a distinguished personal exploration of the North Atlantic triangle.

I am also glad to be able to record my debt to a number of colleagues who were good enough to read the manuscript in whole or in part: to Dr. G. S. R. Kitson Clark, Fellow of Trinity College, Cambridge; Dr. R. K. Webb of Columbia University, who read chapters three and four against the background of his unique knowledge of Harriet Martineau; Dr. John Walsh of Jesus College, Oxford; and Mr. G. A. Shepperson of Edinburgh University. These have saved me from many errors of fact and judgment and for any which remain I am solely responsible. I should also like to thank the members of my seminar at the University of Pennsylvania: Dolores Barracano, Helene S. Benson, Eunice A. Clark, Alexander L. Murray, Maurice R. O'Connell, and Dietmar Röthermund who, American, Canadian, Irish, and German, helped me to plot Atlantic cross currents and allowed me to try out these ideas on them. I owe much to a generous research grant from the Rockefeller Foundation, to the hospitality of the Institute for Advanced Study at Princeton, of which I was a member for the Fall Term, 1954, and to the courtesy of librarians, especially at the Yale and Princeton University libraries, the New York Public Library, and the Library of Friends' House, London. Mrs. Lea Iselin was of great assistance in preparing the manuscript for the press.

F. T.

St. John's College,
  Cambridge,
    October 8, 1958

Contents

AMERICA
AND THE
ATLANTIC
COMMUNITY

Anglo-American
Aspects, 1790-1850

1. The Economic Relation

H AD John Bull and Brother Jonathan, in the early nineteenth century, felt able to look candidly upon each other, they would have recognized that, despite their political animosities, the United States and Britain were more intimately connected than any two other sovereign states. *The Times,* which in those days was no friend to the Americans, put its finger on the matter on the Fourth of July in the year of the Great Exhibition:

For all practical purposes the United States are far more closely united with this kingdom than any one of our colonies, and [with us, they] keep up a perpetual interchange of the most important good offices: taking our manufactures and our surplus population and giving us in return the materials of industry, of revenue and of life.[1]

If the United States was especially important for Britain in an age when British enterprise was carving an economic empire in South America, Africa, India, and the Far East, as well as in Europe and North America, how much more important was Great Britain for the young American Republic! Economically, it is impossible to assess the growth of either country except in relation to the other.

It is historically fruitful to think, not of two separate economies, British and American, but of a single, Atlantic economy.[2]

The American Revolution had not fundamentally altered economic relations, however radically the political relation had altered. The Atlantic traffic of trade and migration had been only temporarily interrupted by the upheaval of the American and French Wars. Although Americans had renounced their allegiance to the British King they could not disentangle themselves from that intricate web of relations across the ocean which had sustained them on the new continent since the first settlements. However persistent their feud with the mother country, however determined to insulate themselves from the European world's slow stain, Americans were unable to withdraw into economic isolation; and they accepted whatever trading terms they could get with the British Empire. The British, for their part, having finally recognized an independent republic in North America, made the best of it by annexing the United States, along with the South American republics, to their informal trading empire. Canning's famous proposal for a joint declaration warning the European Powers off the Atlantic world was based on a shrewd understanding of the potentialities of Anglo-American co-operation, and fitted the facts of economic strategy in the Atlantic better than the unilateral Monroe Doctrine which followed from his initiative. It was not just that without the co-operation of the Royal Navy, that Doctrine was little more than a rhetorical flourish. Old kingdom and new republic shared an unprecedented community of interests.[3]

This community of interests began with a complementary exchange of raw materials for manufactures, which ensured that Britain and the United States should be each other's best customer, in an age when overseas trade, for the United States especially, provided the principal nourishment for economic growth. The relation was not, however, simply that of trade between two closed economies. Political economists as different in outlook as John Stuart Mill, Edward Gibbon Wakefield, and Karl Marx considered the United States, along with the British colonies, to have a special connection with the

United Kingdom outside the normal definition of international trade: a matter, rather, of inter-regional relations within a single economy embracing the entire Atlantic basin.[4]

The essential feature of this special relation, which makes it appropriate to think in such terms, was this. The growth of the Atlantic basin was conditioned, not merely by trade, but by a flow of what economists call the factors of production across the Atlantic into more profitable relations with markets and natural resources. Capital, labor, enterprise, and technology moved west, on a vast scale, and with unique facility, to new American land. That phenomenal twin migration of peoples and of confidence deserves more than the glancing treatment it usually receives at the hands of general historians; it is the central fact of American growth and it relates, not merely to American, but to Atlantic expansion, to a single Atlantic economy.[5]

In the early nineteenth century, the United States was what in modern jargon would be called an "under-developed country," characterized by a plenitude of land and natural resources, but lacking the capital, the techniques, and, in this case, the labor to develop them. The land was rich and seemingly limitless. It could become a cornucopia of farm produce, of raw cotton and wheat, of beef and pork, such as was increasingly in demand in Western Europe where urban populations provided expanding markets for cheap clothing and provisions. But to subdue the wilderness needed more strong arms, more hatchets, knives and clothing, more plows, machinery and hardware, better breeds of cattle, sheep and crops, more canals and railways, than Americans could command. These resources, in terms of emigrant labor, technical skills, durable and consumers' goods, commercial credits, and long-term investment capital, had to be provided from abroad, from the more fully developed countries of Western Europe where there was a surplus of labor released from the land, technical skills, and accumulated capital ready for investment overseas. American growth was determined by the European demand for primary commodities, combined with the European supply of those resources which made their increasing production possible. The American frontier was, in a real sense, one of the frontiers of Europe.[6] The concept has economic meaning, not as a romantic "frontier" of settlement, but as the exploitation of virgin land in a single diversified, Atlantic economy.

In that economy, Western Europe very largely meant a rapidly industrializing Great Britain, with its demand for raw cotton, timber, and foodstuffs, its growing urban population and its rapidly accumulating capital in the hands of risk-taking entrepreneurs. The Atlantic economy was, in fact, characterized by relations between a "metropolitan unit," chiefly Great Britain, and a "colonial" unit, North America, chiefly the United States.[7] Until the frontier of settlement reached the High Plains, an informal Anglo-American partnership continued to direct the growth of the Atlantic basin. If the Americans benefited from British, as well as continental, aid, the British people found in North America an important means of adjusting to the conditions of modern industrial society.

The ancient facts of economic geography continued to determine Atlantic growth. The settlement of the American interior merely shifted the field of operations westwards. The conflict between a continental and an Atlantic outlook, between the perimeter and the base, the province and the metropolis, is as old as the history of America itself. This conflict set up important tensions contributing to the American Revolution. The success of that Revolution did not remove those tensions; political control might shift from Whitehall and Westminster to Philadelphia and the Potomac; but when the United States herself began to colonize, her seaboard cities inherited the role hitherto performed by Britain. And if, with emancipation from Britain, political control shifted across the Atlantic, the British by no means abdicated all their functions in this great westward movement. In the economic, and, as will be seen, to some extent in the cultural sphere, they continued to play the role of a sleeping partner.

More specifically, this partnership was between British interests and American interests of the eastern seaboard. It was, in fact, an Atlantic affair. So integrated was the Atlantic economy, that it is tempting to draw the boundary between its two great regions, not at the Atlantic Ocean, but at the Appalachians. It would be inaccurate to think of the British as contributing directly to the settlement of the Mississippi Valley. Few emigrants had the temperament, capital, or skill to survive the back country, and the native settler's credit and supplies were provided within the United States. But these were made available by the inflow to the eastern seaboard of British commercial credits and investment capital, of immigrant labor shipped by the agencies of British trade routes, and of British immigrant technicians. The force behind continental expansion derived from an oceanic partnership in which New York and Liverpool, Boston and London, New England and northern Old England, together supplied the energy and confidence behind the westward thrust.

In this study we are concerned with the period chiefly between the War of 1812 and the American Civil War when the partnership was in its most active and simple form. It is in many respects a finite period; for at its close the economy was already finding its way toward a new equilibrium. With the decades, the Americans took an increasing hold on the great continental interior, and the American sector of the economy became less "colonial" and more "metropolitan." The nature of the partnership altered until, with American industrialization and the virtual completion of the settlement process in the last quarter of the century, it ceased to be a significant factor in American growth. Already at the time of the Civil War the American sector was achieving an autonomy which makes 1860 a suitable terminal point for this investigation.

Between the Battles of New Orleans and Bull Run, certain specific conditions contributed to the unity and the astonishing growth of the Atlantic economy. In the first place, the institutional framework of the United States made for rapid economic development. The Federal System, grounded on assumptions of limited government, gave remarkably free play to economic forces; and, despite the instability of particular State governments, proved attractive to foreign investors. The Americans were ambitious, acquisitive, and relatively mobile both in an occupational and a geographic sense. The United States was a fair field for capitalism.

In the second place, the obstacles to commercial intercourse across the Atlantic were progressively removed. Trade barriers were relaxed. A long period of low American tariffs provided few deterrents to British manufactures. The United States was admitted to full trading privileges in the British West Indies in 1830, and other British discriminations were gradually reduced until, in 1849, with the abolition of the corn laws and the remnants of the Navigation Code, a climate of relatively free trade blew warm winds across the Atlantic. From 1825 onward the British raised the ban on the export of artisans and of machinery, and British emigration policy shifted from discouragement to indifference which matched that of the United States. Radical improvements in shipping and communications cut the cost of Atlantic travel and helped to integrate commercial and banking practice. Trade and investment were relatively free from government interference.[8] For a quarter of a century the Atlantic economy enjoyed the benefits of laissez-faire which allowed trade, emigrants, and capital to follow, not the flag, but economic opportunity. The greatest single field for British overseas enterprise lay on the western side of the Atlantic, and south of the Forty-ninth Parallel.

Within this framework the Atlantic economy developed in response to the European demand for American primary products. In particular, it was the demand for cotton and wheat which successively determined the growth of markets, the use of land, the flow of credits and capital, and of emigrants. During our period cotton was far and away the more important, a major innovation in the Schumpeterian sense, determining the entire thrust of the Atlantic economy. The demand of Lancashire for raw cotton settled the Southwest, and British commercial credits and investment capital underwrote the Cotton Kingdom. In turn the demand of plantations for provisions encouraged the settlement of the Northwest as a wheat, corn, and hog raising region. At this point, about mid-century, wheat began to take over the running from cotton. The building of canals, largely with British capital, linked the Northwest by the Great Lakes to the East, and made its wheat lands accessible to urban markets and, potentially, to Europe. This potentiality, realized first at the time of the Irish famine of 1846–47, led in the fifties to the building of a railway network, linking the Northwest to the ports. The attractive opportunities of railways, particularly in areas where their very agency would make possible commercial farming, profitable freights and rising land values, induced a new draft of continental and British capital for their construction. This investment ultimately fructified in the great volume of American farm products destined for European markets in the 1870's and eighties. In each of the two great cycles of business activity with which this period is concerned, the first dominated by cotton, the second by wheat, British capital is found playing a leading role. Further, British credits enabled the Americans to import more consumers' goods than they could pay for, and thereby enabled them to divert resources to the long-term exploitation of the Mississippi Valley without suffering the demoralizing effects of inflation and collapse. Although local and domestic initiative started the cotton boom of the thirties and the prairie land boom of the fifties, the confidence of foreign investors prevented those booms from petering out and sustained them over a number of years. The key to American growth before the Civil War must be sought in European, and largely British, markets, European, and again largely British, capital resources; in other words, in the dynamics of an Atlantic economy.[9]

This theme will be developed by examining the three major topics involved, namely, trade, the migration of capital, and the migration of labor.

In focusing on one aspect of the trade of both countries, one must not ignore other aspects of the Atlantic trading community. For Britain, the American was only one, although the most important, of several overseas markets. As for the United States, a half-century of independence had permitted the exploitation of numerous profitable markets, notably in the Mediterranean, China, India and South America, which contributed in important ways to the balancing of her international payments. Having called attention to this, however, one is justified in concentrating on the Anglo-American trade, in view of its primary importance in stimulating the growth of both countries.

Between the Treaty of Ghent and the Civil War the United States was Britain's chief customer and the Americans were largely dependent on Britain for their textiles, hardware, iron, indeed for most of their manufactures. Britain was the United States' chief market and the most valuable part of America's agricultural surplus found its way to British ports. Between 1820 and 1860 nearly half American exports went to Britain, whence came about 40 per cent of American imports.[10] Of foreign tonnage entering American ports in 1860, four-fifths was British.

Such bald figures, though impressive, do not convey the full importance of Anglo-American trade. In terms of innovation, that pulsating artery across the North Atlantic takes on a heightened significance. Its most nutritive element was the textiles which, in Professor Albion's words, "towered above all else in the world of commerce of that day." The cotton bale was the most important article in American commerce.[11] In the thirty years after 1821 the value of raw cotton in American exports rose from nearly 40 per cent to nearly 60 per cent, dwarfing its nearest rivals, flour and tobacco, which constituted not more than ten per cent each. In 1860 cotton exports paid for three-fifths of American imports.[12] Raw cotton was also the most valuable item in British imports, and 80 per cent of it came from the Southern States.[13]

The cotton trade was not just a one-way affair. Finished textiles were Britain's chief article of export, some 60 per cent of the whole. Textiles were the most important of American imports, about a third of the whole. The proportion of cotton cloth in this total declined with the growth of domestic industry; but throughout the period, just over 90 per cent of American woollen and just under 90 per cent of American cotton imports came from Britain.[14] Cotton was the most important stimulus to growth in both countries. The Cotton

Kingdom was not limited to the Old South; its frontiers extended across the Atlantic to Lancashire and the Clyde, and its influence quickened the entire Atlantic world. Cotton gin and slave plantation were linked with spinning frame and power loom as constituent elements in a single innovation.

The cotton trade confirmed the Atlantic pre-eminence of Liverpool which drew away from Bristol and London to become the chief entrepôt of American trade even before the abolition of the slave trade struck at her earlier staple in 1807. The port possessed a magnificent harbor, accessible to Irish ports and by means of canals and railways to the woollens of the West Riding, the cutlery of Sheffield, the iron of the Black Country, the hardware of Birmingham and the pottery of Staffordshire, as well as the cottons of Lancashire.[15] By 1820 two-thirds of the British shipping bound for the United States sailed from the Mersey.[16] Liverpool merchants developed an extensive trade with the United States and established close connections with Philadelphian and New York houses.[17] This network of merchants and brokers was supplemented by British manufacturers who sold direct to American wholesalers. Agents of Staffordshire potters and Sheffield and Birmingham hardware manufacturers had established themselves in New York by the 1820's. More important were the cotton and woollen goods salesmen from the Pennines who, as Professor Heaton has shown, had already opened counting houses on New York's Pearl Street before the War of 1812.[18] After the Peace, when British merchants chose New York as the port on which to unload the contents of their overstocked warehouses, these agents played a central role in developing the New York-Liverpool axis and in establishing the pre-eminence of New York. For New York, in turn, with her superb harbor, the hinterland annexed by her great canal, and her Liverpool connections, became the greatest importing port in the United States and entrepôt for the trade in raw cotton from the South.[19]

Chief among these British agents were the Thompson family. At the turn of the century, Francis and Jeremiah Thompson, uncle and nephew of a Quaker, manufacturing family at Rawdon in the West Riding of Yorkshire, crossed the Atlantic to sell their firm's woollens. Francis married the daughter of a Long Island Quaker, Isaac Wright, and with his father-in-law and nephew became a dry goods importer and ship-owner. After the War of 1812, the Thompsons used their English connections to become one of the leading houses in the North Atlantic trade; and Jeremiah, especially, became one of its creative entrepreneurs.[20]

In 1818 the Thompson firm made an important innovation in ocean trade. There had recently been developments in the sailing powers of ships; they were more economical to build, had larger cargo space, and were capable of being handled with smaller crews; they were also faster, and sailing nearer the wind, were able to reach port more regularly. Taking advantage of these improvements the Thompsons decided to employ three modern vessels, not, like the "regular traders," on independent voyages, but as a "packet" line with announced times of departure, like the British admiralty mailboats. From January 4, when the *Courier* cleared Liverpool for New York, the Black Ball Line maintained regular fortnightly sailings on the North Atlantic run. The striking success of this innovation, which Professor Albion regards as an important cause of the ascendancy of New York, quickly led to the formation of other lines from New York, Philadelphia, and Boston to British and continental ports.[21] The Atlantic voyage was shortened by a quarter between 1830 and 1850; and with the advent of the clipper, which did all that a sailing ship could do, these times were cut still further. Donald

McKay's *Lightning* once covered 436 miles of the Liverpool
run in twenty-four hours. The arrival in New York Bay on
St. George's Day, 1838, of the steamer *Sirius* and, within a
few hours, of a second steamer, *Great Western,* was the signal
for yet another improvement in the voyage through the black
waters of the North Atlantic.[22] The speed and regular de-
livery of cargo and mail, both by sail and steam, revolutionized business correspondence, market intelligence, and the
stability of prices. Cabin passages were cheaper and more
comfortable. What had been an adventure, even an ordeal,
became a habitual routine, not only for businessmen, but for
travelers of all kinds. The two shores of the Atlantic were
brought closer together; and people talked excitedly about
one Atlantic world in much the same terms as their air-
minded descendants talked of One World.

As a result of his shipping ventures, Jeremiah Thompson
had become by 1827 one of the largest shipowners in the
United States.[23] This led him to take the lead in a second
innovation. In order to find suitable cargo to fill his east-
bound ships, he began to trade in raw cotton. Another partner, Benjamin Marshall, Huddersfield-born but trained in
the Lancashire cotton manufacture, spent his winters in
Georgia buying up cotton crops on the plantation. The bales
were then shipped to New York and transshipped into
Thompson vessels bound for Liverpool where they were sold
to pay for the British dry goods, some of which, in turn, were
sold South. By 1827 Jeremiah Thompson was the most extensive cotton dealer in the world, with an annual turnover of
some 150,000 bales.[24] To him is due the principal credit for
developing that "cotton triangle" which ensured that New
York should obtain the profits, and suffer the risks, of han-
dling the greater part of the South's cotton crop.[25]

Cotton dealing, in those days of private partnerships and

wild price fluctuations, was highly speculative; and for all its credit resources the Thompson house became over-extended. In the crisis of 1827 Jeremiah's drafts were refused by Cropper, Benson and Co., his Liverpool correspondents, and the whole Thompson edifice, including the parent manufacturing firm at Rawdon, collapsed.[26] This did not, however, put an end to the creative activities of the Thompson family. Francis ran an immigrant business which his nephew Samuel developed into a regular line of immigrant packets, the Union Line. Hitherto, British emigrants to North America had largely traveled as return between-decks cargo in the timber and cotton merchantmen which had unloaded at Liverpool, Belfast, or other ports. The potentialities of this human cargo were exploited in an organized trade by Liverpool passenger brokers who contracted to supply cargoes of emigrants just as others contracted to supply railway iron. Before the New York immigrant regulations of the 1840's, and the British Passenger Acts of the fifties, the trade was notorious for the overcrowding and hardships suffered by immigrants. There is no evidence that the Thompsons were motivated by the Quakerly philanthropy which they displayed elsewhere; but the use of special emigrant ships and packet lines helped to cure this black spot in the North Atlantic trade.

The career of Jeremiah Thompson epitomizes the central dynamic of the Atlantic economy. Armed with Yorkshire cloth to sell, with expert knowledge of the trade, with Liverpool credit, he bridged the Atlantic, and helped make New York the paramount port, not only for importing British manufactures, but for exporting and eventually controlling the South's great cotton staple. By his shipping innovations he brought New York closer to Liverpool, and made it easier for European emigrants to follow the trade route to the New World. Thompson is one of those rare entrepreneurs who enable one to go behind statistics and theory to discover economic history as the decisions of creative individuals.

The Thompsons were, however, only among the more prominent of the British trading fraternity in the American Atlantic ports, a few in Baltimore, more in Philadelphia, but most congregating in New York. Many of them remained manufacturer's agents, disposing of their goods through the New York auctions and lodging in the many boarding houses which catered to the British community.[27] But some were more substantial. In 1846 over sixty residents in the city who were British-born or of immediate British descent, had fortunes of $100,000 or more.[28] Such fortunes were made from a miscellany of trades: shipbuilding, paper manufacture, sugar and candymaking, bookselling and newspaper publishing, pills, wholesale groceries, retail store keeping as well as, in some cases, from marrying heiresses. Most, however, were made in the import trade. Some handled iron from the Black Country and Wales; others hardware from Birmingham, earthenware from the potteries, coal from South Wales and Lancashire; but the great majority dealt in textiles: Irishmen from Belfast in linens, Lancastrians in cottons, Yorkshiremen in woollens, Scotsmen in carpets, and one James Chesterman, a tailor of Bolton, Lancashire, pioneered in the import of those ready-to-wear suits which were to induce a typically American utility demand.[29] These dry goods merchants, "the damned Yorkshiremen," the "drab-gaitered tykes" of the protectionist Hezekiah Niles, with their counting houses on Pearl Street or South Street, were a key element in the North Atlantic trade, and they act as tracers in the growing complexity of commercial operations.[30] Some, like the Thompsons, became important shipowners; some, as we shall see, used their credit resources and knowledge to become merchant bankers; others went into insurance, like Henry Eyre who directed the New York branch of the Royal Insurance Company of Liverpool.[31] Alexander T. Stewart and the Sloanes, father and son, entered the retail trade and developed prosperous dry goods stores on Broadway.[32] Still others made another characteristic transition. In 1824 Benjamin Marshall shifted from trading in raw cotton and textiles to cotton manufacturing, and his factory at Troy was among the first to make fine cottons in the United States.[33] James Boorman progressed from importing railway iron to pioneering the Hudson River Railroad, Charles Cartlidge from importing earthenware to becoming a successful potter himself at Greenpoint, Long Island.[34] These men, like Jeremiah Thompson, were key entrepreneurs in the Atlantic economy: the merchant-turned-industrialist, the emigrant who helped establish industry on the western Atlantic shores.

The British merchants in New York and Philadelphia formed distinct fraternities. Like other British communities-in-exile from Calcutta to Buenos Aires, they regarded Britain as home. Some became naturalized; but most seem to have remained British subjects and looked forward to retiring to the old country. A few actually did so. Thomas Dixon returned to Eastbourne during the Civil War with a fortune from the dry goods trade and E. F. Sanderson, a cutlery importer, retired similarly fortified to Sheffield.[35] But these were probably exceptional. Most died in the city or its suburbs, and some of the more wealthy left sizeable bequests to New York University, the New York Public Library and to mechanics institutes, Bible and tract societies, and hospitals. They were "middle-class" communities. In New York they tended to live in the then fashionable Greenwich Village district, in Park Place or Beekman Street, although James Chesterman built himself a *château à l'Anglais* in the bosky suburb of Harlem. They subscribed to periodicals like the *Albion* and the *Anglo-American,* which combined local British news with literary essays, and comment derived from British periodicals.[36] Their political views about American affairs in the Age of Jackson were decidedly "Whiggish" and conservative. If they could afford it, they joined the Albion Club in Park Place and supported the friendly societies of St. George, St. Andrew and St. David, which dined on their saint's day at Delmonico's or Niblo's Saloon.[37] They celebrated the Queen's birthday with oyster parties on Staten Island; and cricket clubs in New York and Philadelphia exchanged matches.[38] These communities kept themselves, in a measure, apart from American life. In the words of a shrewd contemporary observer of emigration and of Anglo-American relations:

It should be noted that Englishmen, when, in rare cases, they become naturalized, usually vote with the once aristocratic party, and seldom if ever on the same side with the Irish. However, few Englishmen residing in America renounce their allegiance to their own Government. They are patriotic John Bulls. They take British papers, frequent British beer-houses, drink British ale, and are proud and happy to call themselves "British residents." [39]

In the Atlantic community, their role was not that of emigrants. Rather it was to establish a bridgehead for the promotion of Anglo-American trade, a bridgehead, based on the home land, which was to enable others to bring their brawn, brains, and skills, as genuine emigrants to American society. These will be referred to later.

The North Atlantic trade was not by any means exclusively in the hands of the British merchant houses. By the 1830's British merchants in New York had come to be balanced by American merchants in Liverpool and London; and an American Chamber of Commerce existed in Liverpool from 1801; [40] but the membership was English and the trade continued to be dominated by the British. Americans, by the nature of their colonizing circumstances, were short of capital and interest rates were high. The British, as a result of a century of mercantile enterprise and the profits of industrialization, possessed ample investable funds. American merchants, therefore, could not compete with the low interest rates and long credit terms, often eighteen months, offered by their British rivals. American, as well as British, houses were supported by commercial credit deriving from the powerful London money market. This British backing not only financed North Atlantic commerce and American trade with the Far East, but sustained a channel of credit, through New York jobbers and country wholesalers to remote storekeepers, farmers, and planters, which made possible a rapid expansion of the continental hinterland. In 1837 the amount of this credit outstanding was estimated at about one hundred million dollars. [41]

This credit was provided by a transatlantic network of about seven merchant banking houses. A number of these began as dry goods merchants in the American trade, and some continued to combine the dual functions of merchant and banker. Alexander Brown and Sons, later Brown Brothers, had its origins in County Antrim, Ireland, whence in 1798 Alexander Brown, a linen merchant, emigrated to Baltimore to establish a warehouse for the sale of linens. His sons, who were educated in England, were taken into partnership. William, established in 1809 in a branch in Liverpool (later Brown, Shipley, and Company), remained British, became an alderman of Liverpool, a Member of Parliament, a baronet, and a great benefactor to his city. George remained with his father in Baltimore; John became head of a branch in Philadelphia (later Brown, Harriman, and Company),

James, in 1825, of a branch in New York. The firm expanded
from linen to general merchandise, and built up a merchant
banking business. The importance of Brown Brothers' London connections is indicated by the fact that although in the
panic of 1837 the firm was caught over-extended, they managed to negotiate with the Bank of England a credit of two
million pounds, and survived with an enhanced reputation.
Thenceforward the linen trade was abandoned, and the house
devoted itself exclusively to merchant banking and exchange
business.[42] Three other houses, Wilson, Wildes and Wiggin
—the famous "Three W's"—who failed in the same crisis,
were of London origin. George Peabody, however, was a New
England dry goods merchant with a business in Baltimore
and branches in Philadelphia and New York. In 1837 he went
to London where he gradually extended the business of
George Peabody and Company (later J. S. Morgan and Company) from merchandising to merchant banking. By the time
of the Civil War he was the outstanding American agent in
London, an important philanthropist, and a public figure in
the City, of which he was given the freedom, despite remain-
ing an American citizen and refusing a title. There is a
statue of him near the Royal Exchange.[43] The most powerful
house was Baring Brothers of London which, though long
established in other markets, concentrated on the American.
With great financial resources, with the American connections of Alexander Baring (later Lord Ashburton) who married a Philadelphia Bingham, with the operational dexterity
in London of Joshua Bates, a New Englander from Wey-
mouth, Massachusetts, and of their American agent, Thomas
Ward, the Barings weathered all financial crises and, along
with the Rothschilds, had the lion's share in marketing American securities in Europe.[44]

For the role of Anglo-American merchant bankers went beyond commercial credit. By marketing in London the bonds of the Southern States, which were used to finance State banks, the Anglo-American houses enabled London to underwrite the development of cotton lands in the Deep South. In 1838 the bonds of the Cotton States were a third of all State securities; and about half of them, some eighty-six million, were held in England.[45] Nor did British investors limit themselves to the Cotton Kingdom. In England after Waterloo discerning people, believing in the future material prosperity of the American republic, sought opportunities for investment there. The old British aristocratic habit of buying American land persisted, and may be traced in each phase of the western advance. The young Alexander Baring was investing heavily in tracts on the Penobscot in Maine as early as 1795.[46] In 1790, the Pulteney family, Marquises of Bath, secured 1,300,000 acres of the Phelps, Gorham tract in the Genesee Valley in western New York, and, with the Wadsworth family, shared in the development of that fertile region of the Finger Lakes.[47] The charms of James Wadsworth's daughter led Sir Charles Augustus Murray to contemplate American citizenship and to acquire twenty thousand acres in Wisconsin during the land boom there in the 1830's. His suit was unsuccessful and he returned to Britain to a career as courtier and diplomat; but his gesture is one of the links between the eighteenth century and the late nineteenth century mania by British landed magnates to invest in western cattle estates.[48]

These were individual ventures. Most British funds found their way to the United States as a result of the marketing by the Anglo-American houses of American securities in London. The bonds of the Federal Government found a ready and early sale in England. However, the greatest avenue of British investment was into American State and, to a less extent, municipal securities of which, in 1853, 58 per cent and 23 per cent respectively were held in Europe.[49] This represents in some ways the most significant contribution to American growth. For apart from the State banks, largely Southern, this money went overwhelmingly into the State and municipal financed turnpikes, canals, and railways, those "internal improvements" in transport so essential to commercial development which required drafts of capital on a scale far beyond the means of this very under-developed country. An English country gentleman may have been impressed merely by an imposing State seal and ten per cent interest; but his banker was aware of the potentialities of the American west. The shining example of the Erie Canal, the stock of which rapidly found its way to England, induced visions of rich and profitable crops of wheat brought by canal and the Great Lakes to markets on the eastern seaboard and in Europe. The mania to buy canal and railway stock was, in fact, only a new variant of the old urge to speculate in land. Between 1821 and 1837 foreign capital to the value of about 125 million dollars, most of it British, was invested in the United States.[50]

The canal boom came and went; but the attraction of railways persisted. From the early days of the *Baltimore and Ohio* and the *Camden and Amboy*, British funds played a major role in building American railways. Often local capital provided land and roadbed; but the builders of a number of pioneer roads turned to South Wales for their railway iron for which they often paid in the bonds of their company. By this means, as well as by direct flotation, American railway securities found their way to the City of London where, by the middle fifties, there was active trading in American rails. Important roads such as the *New York Central*, the *Erie*, the *Pennsylvania*, the *Michigan Central* and the *Illinois Central*, obtained decisive capital in Britain and, in a few cases, Amer-

ican railways were controlled by committees of security hold-
ers in London. During the fifties nearly two hundred million
dollars worth of new investment capital flowed into the United
States, mostly into railways; in 1860 British and European investment in the country was estimated at four hundred million dollars, which was probably more than 20 per cent of the
total funded indebtedness.[51] Considering that it had made
possible the great railway boom of the preceding years, it was
a fraction of great significance.

The greater part of this money was invested in enterprise
which would strengthen the Atlantic economy: to finance
trade and agriculture and to build the transport network
which would link a continental market to the Atlantic trade
routes. These were the overriding needs for which Americans
sought European help. Little British capital seems to have
been invested directly in the infant American industries,
which were locally financed and which British capitalists no
doubt considered both to be risky and to challenge the markets of British industry. British investment appears to have
reflected a belief in a United States of boundless agricultural
and mineral wealth which should remain a complementary
partner to an industrialized Britain. The economy benefited,
not only from the size of the foreign investment, but from
the experienced guidance which the Anglo-American merchant bankers brought to the problems of American development. Writing of the Barings, two American historians
have called attention to the leading strings of the American
economy which were held in metropolitan London:

. . . we were able to borrow the precious capital of the British
for both commercial and investment purposes. But beyond these
splendid advantages we experienced the steadying hand of wise
and beneficent bankers who would help America grow, but not
too fast and not too dangerously.[52]

The movement of labor bears little direct relation to that of capital. Only the exceptional British firm established an American branch, like the British-owned Mount Savage Ironworks in Allegheny County, Maryland, which rolled the first heavy iron rails in the United States.[53] Apart from the accidental cases of an Irish navvy or a Scots railway engineer, British emigrants did not normally take up occupations in the United States which were financed by British investors. Yet, the swelling of the American population beyond the natural rate of increase by an influx of immigrants created a buoyant market for industry and commerce; and without that stimulant, European capital would not have been attracted to the United States on any scale. According to Professor Brinley Thomas, emigration may have been the leading factor in economic growth in this period, and successive waves of emigration sometimes may have been in advance of those of investment capital.[54]

However, if the connection with capital was indirect that with trade was close. Emigrants, like timber or cotton, were bulk cargo; the great migration from Europe was an aspect of commerce and followed the trade routes. Even when, in the fifties, the source of emigrants shifted eastwards to Germany and Scandinavia, many of the later voyagers reached New York or New Orleans by way of British ports.[55] Without these pre-existing trade routes migration could hardly have gathered momentum. For it took place without the benefit of government aid or organization: it was a piecemeal affair of individual decision and adventure.

The motives for migration were as various as the types of individuals. A few, who will be discussed in subsequent chapters, sought freedom for political or religious principle; but such motives are statistically unmeasurable. Judging by figures alone, most Britons went in search of an opportunity which, although it had social implications, was basically economic. The existence of the North Atlantic trade routes made labor geographically mobile at a time when in the metropolitan country labor was comparatively immobile in an occupational and class sense, and when rapid technological change and violent oscillations in the trade cycle made for the chronic displacement of industrial and farm workers.[56] The line of least resistance for the unemployed farm laborer or cotton operative, was often, not to change his trade, or even to seek work in another British center, but to pursue that trade by canal, train, and ship across the Atlantic where land was cheap and skilled labor commanded high wages. In addition, there was the attraction of a new country, with a relatively high degree of occupational and social mobility, together with the more intangible, but nonetheless real, hope of betterment under republican institutions. In other words, within the Atlantic economy, it was often easier for a working man to move from one region to another even if this meant crossing the ocean, rather than to make an even more painful adjustment at home. Many returned, disillusioned; many artisans made a practice of voyaging to and fro across the Atlantic in the practice of their trade, either seasonally or in accordance with the relative demand for their services in the western or eastern sector of the economy. We do not know how many returned: but many, in the end, remained and adjusted to life in the New World.

Such were the conditions which encouraged more than half the emigrants from the British Isles between 1815 and 1840 to choose the United States.[57] An increasing proportion of these emigrants were, it is true, the Irish, who had special reasons for their choice; but in 1860 there were in the United States nearly six hundred thousand persons who had been born in England, Scotland or Wales, and these represented some 14 per cent of the total foreign-born population of the country.[58]

How did these immigrants fare in their adopted country? What did their uprooting contribute to the Atlantic economy? Although for this period statistics are poor there exists enough qualitative evidence of particular groups of individuals to draw certain conclusions.

First, they did not settle in the South. The trade routes carried them by ship, steamboat, canal, and railway to northern ports, or perhaps to New Orleans, and thence inland to the Northwest: the slave economy offered no opportunities to the free white worker who, in any case, shrank from slavery.

Second, a sizeable number persevered with the ambition to settle on the land. From the 1790's onwards, in each stage of American settlement, British immigrants are to be found staking out homesteads and grubbing up trees: on the Susquehanna after the War of 1812, in western New York and Illinois in the twenties, in Michigan and Wisconsin in the thirties and forties. Emigrant letters and diaries reveal them, sometimes clinging to a neighborhood of English, Welsh, or Scots, but struggling, like their Yankee or Southern neighbors, with the intractable problems of the back-country. A very few, like the Birkbecks of Illinois, were men of substance, with capital enough to sink in clearing an extensive tract.[59] But most were humble people. The most successful were countrymen like the Burlends of Barwick-in-Elmet, Yorkshire, in Illinois, or the Muirs, of Dunbar, in Wisconsin.[60] Some of the artisans survived in the wilderness, like the Bottomleys of Huddersfield, in Wisconsin; [61] but as a class they were notorious for their incompetence on the frontier, and they were prominent among those British migrants whom travellers reported making a disgusted return journey to the seaboard. Of the few organized emigration schemes, three came to grief in the 1840's partly because of the incompetence of town-bred artisans: one a community of Staffordshire potters in Wisconsin, the second, a semi-philanthropic venture by the Liverpool Temperance Emigration Society, also in Wisconsin, the third, a settlement of artisans and tradesmen from Hull in Iowa.[62] But despite many failures, the flotsam of strange, broken characters, a proportion of the British survived the backwoods to grow up with the country. By 1850 some 120,000 British-born lived in the North Central States, about a third of the total British-born in the United States, and the State with the highest percentage of English-born was Wisconsin.[63] These families are difficult to trace, because their ethnic, religious, and social backgrounds enabled them to "pass," so to speak, more easily than the Scandinavians and Germans into the dominant Yankee social milieu.[64] Some became forceful leaders in their communities: prosperous farmers, merchants, bankers, doctors, and clergy. Some even became politicians, like the Scotsman William E. Smith who graduated from the wholesale hardware and grocery business to the State legislature and ultimately to the Governorship of Wisconsin, whence he retired to his native Scotland.[65] A few emerged among the first, largely native-born, generation of thrusting business leaders. Take the joint careers of George Smith and Alexander Mitchell. Smith was a Scottish farmer who emigrated in 1834. He intended to farm, but instead used his capital to launch an insurance and banking business in Chicago and then in Milwaukee. To manage the latter in 1838 he brought in another emigrant just arrived from Aberdeen, Alexander Mitchell. Mitchell expanded his banking activities until he became the greatest financial power in the growing State of Wisconsin. From banking he went into railways, and built an empire of small roads reaching out to St. Paul which ensured that the business of this

area reached the east via Milwaukee, whose leading citizen
he had become by the time of the Civil War. He is included
by Miss Gregory and Miss Neu in their analysis of the American industrial élite of the 1870's.[66]

Such immigrants made a contribution to American growth
which far outweighed their numbers. This was also true of
the other main group of British, who bulk so large in the
total, the artisans and mechanics.

In 1850, half the British-born were to be found in the seaboard States of New York, Pennsylvania and Massachusetts; [67]
and a sixth went to swell the rapidly growing population of
the ports of Boston, New York, Philadelphia and Baltimore.[68]
Of the port-dwellers, some were shopkeepers and traders,
some, laborers on the docks and in warehouses and *abattoirs.*
Nearly 20 per cent of the Scots and about 14 per cent of the
English and Welsh in New York worked in the building
trades as masons, bricklayers, and carpenters, and about ten
per cent of the English and Scots in the clothing trades.[69]
Some were migrants, although few could have used the Atlantic trade route as systematically as those house painters
who worked in America in the spring, in Scotland in the
summer before English families went north, and in England
in the autumn while the shooting season was still in progress.[70] Many were highly-skilled craftsmen. Together with
English and Scots cabinet-makers, shipwrights, ship carpenters, riggers, and engineers they formed a distinct community
in New York, reading the *Old Countryman* and the *Scottish
Patriot,* gravitating towards the Brown Jug Tavern, the
Richard the Third, the Blue Bonnet House, a rowdy element,
taking part, as will be seen, in workingmen's politics, and
forming a *claque* for the English actor Macready against the
American, Forrest, which started the Astor Place Riot of
1849.[71]

However, the most significant were those skilled in the new industries of Britain, carriers of the new technology of steam, iron, and machinery, the principal agents in transplanting modern industry from the English midlands and Scotland to the American continent. For American industrialization is best conceived as a process of colonization from the metropolitan, to the undeveloped, sector of the Atlantic economy.

Americans, conditioned by a lack of capital and labor to the reckless exploitation of forests, soils, and ocean, were barely scratching the surface of their continent. It was British immigrant miners, for the most part, who took over the shallow pits of the American amateurs and, with their specialized skills, first burrowed into the seams of mineral wealth. This advance force, "pioneers" in the strict sense of the term, established the basis for the metal-working industries. As early as 1820 tin miners from the Camborne district of Cornwall were working the lead mines of the Galena district on the frontier of the upper Mississippi; later, they and their successors were to open up the great copper and iron beds of Lake Superior and, even after the influx of central European and Finnish miners, to provide the essential *cadre* of mine captains. These "Cousin Jacks" preserved their distinctive way of life, building stone cottages like those of Redruth, cooking Cornish pasties, drinking beer rather than spirits, and speaking the Cornish dialect.[72] From the 1840's onwards coal miners, some from County Durham, Derbyshire, Stafford and South Wales, but more from the Scottish coalfields, tunnelled into the bituminous and anthracite seams of the Alleghenies and later of southern Illinois. These immigrants provided the United States with its first generation of skilled coal miners, constituting a mining aristocracy from whom were recruited mine engineers and managers, State inspectors of mines and trade union leaders.[73] Similar in their skilled

exploitation of American natural resources were the potters
from the Five Towns of Staffordshire. The export trade of
the potteries, like that of cotton-manufacturing Lancashire,
was dominated by the American market; and it proved a natural step for journeymen potters to cross the Atlantic, attracted by the potentialities of their market and the rumor
of the existence of suitable clays. English potters, almost un-
aided either by native capital or skill, established the American potting industry, first in northern New Jersey and Philadelphia, and then at East Liverpool, Ohio, where an itinerant
English potter, James Bennett, fired a kiln of mugs using
local clay and coal in 1839. From such tiny backwoods beginnings there grew a sturdy little industry largely of English
firms which, by the Civil War, was beginning to capture the
coarse pottery market from their cousins and rivals in the
English potteries. The potters, too, like the Cornish and the
Welsh, clung together in tight immigrant communities,
bound by parochial origins and by the loyalties of an eso-
teric craft.[74]

More important than the clay-working industry was the
working of iron. The primitive, charcoal-burning iron trade
was transformed into a vigorous, progressive industry not
only by British techniques but by British technicians. British
iron-founders and furnacemen helped pioneer successive improvements, from the first Pittsburgh rolling mill in 1812,
the hot-blast furnaces and the coke and anthracite smelting
of the Welshman David Thomas and the Englishman William Firmstone in the 1830's and forties, to the first T rails of
Benjamin Haywood and the crucible steel of the Garrard
brothers. On the heels of these creative innovators, several of
whom became successful ironmasters, there travelled scores,
then hundreds of skilled iron workers from the English midlands and more particularly from South Wales. These pro-

vided an essential *cadre* of labor for the American iron trade and contributed to those Welsh-speaking and singing communities which persisted so long in Pennsylvania, Ohio, and elsewhere.[75]

The most important group of industrial immigrants was to be found in the first of the new industries of Britain to be fully established in the United States. From the days of Samuel Slater and the Scholfields, spinners, weavers, calico printers, and machine-makers from Lancashire, the West Riding and Scotland had been quietly and illegally taking ship to sell the new, secret technology in the United States. The technical basis of an American textile industry was established by immigrants from the textile metropolis; and following the original mechanical geniuses who built spinning frames, carding machines, looms, and printing machines, thousands of artisans came to provide an essential stiffening of skills for the labor force in textiles.[76] There was a scattering of British operatives in cotton, woollen, carpet, and silk factories in Philadelphia, New Jersey, and New York; but they congregated especially in the cotton factories of Rhode Island and Massachusetts.[77] The English were an important element even in the essentially "American" mill town of Lowell; [78] but they went to Pawtucket and Fall River in large numbers, traveling direct from Liverpool by packet to New York, some returning after a season of high wages if conditions improved at home, some working out their lives in robust British-American communities which had their St. George's Societies, and their British workingmen's clubs.[79] These cotton operatives like other artisans, brought their work habits. The mule spinners, especially, knew their worth and, stubborn Lancastrians that they were, appear to have made a minimum adjustment to American ways. Their New England employers found them rough, drunken and cantankerous. Perhaps more aware than native-born workers of the nature of modern industrial society, they took the lead in organizing trade unions, strikes and co-operatives.[80] And it was not long before employers looked about for a more docile labor force, Irish and French-Canadian, who could be taught to work machinery.[81] But during our period, the English dominated the cotton industry of southern New England. That is, as workers; for after the first generation, few British-born in textiles appear to have climbed higher than the salaried post of mill superintendent, and most remained in the spinning or weaving shed. Yankee capital was early in the field, and New England merchant families seem to have kept control firmly in their own hands.[82]

This migration of British technicians has a distinctive character. One can discern successive phases: first, the migration of creative innovators, like the Slaters and Scholfields in textiles, the Thomas's, Firmstones, and Crowthers in iron smelting and founding, the Bennetts in potting, the first generation of Cornish mine captains, of Scottish coal miners: these were the carriers of the new technology who made it effective in the new environment; and although their influence varied industry by industry, some achieved the status of entrepreneur or at least of manager. Secondly, close on their heels came the scores and hundreds of skilled operatives who were to provide the essential *cadre* of mule spinners, machine makers, foundrymen and miners, some seasonal migrants only, some settling into communities of British folkways and craft loyalties, and, more conscious than American workers of the nature of modern capitalism, taking the lead in establishing unions. Then there was a third phase, when improved machinery and American production methods reduced the scope of skilled labor and increased the number of jobs which could be handled by cheaper, unskilled and more docile workers recruited from more recent, and non-British immigrant stocks. This is a point which had hardly been reached by the Civil War, except perhaps in textiles where the Irish and French-Canadians were beginning to replace the British. This technical migration was a finite movement. It performed a specific role in the migration of industry from the eastern to the western sectors of the Atlantic economy in pursuit of markets and raw materials.

The foregoing is a sketch of the specific ways in which an informal Anglo-American partnership determined the flow of trade, of capital and of labor within an Atlantic economy. It was a relationship between two complementary regions which transcended the schisms of the political realm. Inter-dependence has been, of course, a normal condition of international relations, at least since the development of modern capitalism; and the Atlantic economy might be said to be only a phase in the growth of what is sometimes called a world economy. Yet the Atlantic economy had a unity, a boldness of definition, of contour, which is perhaps unique. But in the specific sense in which the term has been used the Atlantic economy proved to be only a passing phase in the growth of the region which it embraced.

The economy was subject to wild fluctuations and major maladjustments. As Professor Jenks long ago pointed out, the Anglo-American partnership in the development of the North American continent was too impatient for results, too easily beguiled by State guarantees and ten per cent, too optimistic about the primitive American banking system, too ignorant of political factors, to succeed in its attempt profitably to control the westward movement.[83] Over-extension brought about financial collapse in 1839, which halted western growth for a decade. Anglo-American trade languished, and there was an ebb in the migration of capital and labor. The Jacksonian insurgents attacked, not merely the oligarchs of Chestnut Street, but the sinister influence of British bankers; and the shock in London caused by the defaulting on their bonds by great American States like Pennsylvania, induced a classic case of Anglo-American friction, etched in the acid sarcasm of Sidney Smith: "And now," wrote the man Americans called "The Rev. Shylock Smith," "having eased my soul of its indignation, and sold my stock at 40 per cent discount, I sulkily retire from the subject, with a fixed intention of lending no more money to free and enlightened republics, but of employing my money henceforth in buying up Abyssinian bonds, and purchasing into the Turkish Fours, or the Tunis Three-and-a-half per cent funds."

However, the partnership weathered the crisis, and emerged into the golden sunlight of the 1850's. Trade revived. The flow of emigrants was resumed and increased dramatically in proportions. Not tens, but hundreds of thousands, in 1854 nearly half a million, European emigrants each year crossed the Atlantic to swell the labor force in the eastern cities, in transport and on the farm. In complementary fashion, European capital was once again attracted on a large scale to the exploitation of American lands, chiefly now in the form of railways. Here, though the dominance of cotton in American exports was never so marked as on the eve of the Civil War, interest shifted from the Cotton Belt to the wheat-growing prairies. Ex-China merchants like John Murray Forbes were building railways to tap the rich corn of the Midwest and to link that region with the Northeast as a great commercial empire; and free trade and antislavery advocates as far apart as Ohio and Manchester, England, as we shall see in Chapter Six, were dreaming of replacing slave-cotton by free-grown wheat as the pre-eminent American export. This was a sow-ing which British towns, as well as the immigrant-inflated ports of the United States were to reap in the form of cheap foodstuffs in the 1860's and 1870's. The Anglo-American partnership, based on cotton, persisted into an age of wheat.

Yet there were signs that the old intimacy, with its nice balance of complementary forces, was shaken.

In the first place, by 1865 there had developed a money market in New York which was not only, in a measure, emancipated from Lombard Street, but was becoming integrated directly with the capital markets of the European continent; and a new connection of German-American merchant bankers, dealing with Frankfurt and Amsterdam, supplemented the older Anglo-American banking community.

Secondly, with the increase in the flow of emigrants went a change in its composition. European emigrants continued to make use of trade routes centring on the British Isles; but, although the English, Welsh, and Scots remained, from a technological point of view, a highly significant fraction, they shrank in proportion as other ethnic groups, southern Irish, German, and, later, Scandinavian, swelled the total, and there began that gradual eastward shift in recruitment which is somewhat artificially defined by the distinction between "old" and "new" emigration.

Thirdly, as a result of the Atlantic migration of industry, American manufacturers began to compete with their British rivals for the domestic American market; and the complementary character of the two sectors of the Atlantic economy, based on the exchange of raw materials for manufactures, came to be qualified.

With capital provided by New England merchants which, but for European resources might have been drawn into transport, with British technology, and behind a tariff wall, a textile industry had grown so sturdily that by the 1840's the infant was already showing the parent new tricks. British devices such as the Roberts self-acting mule, continued to be imported; but they were rapidly improved. American inventions, such as ring spinning, automatic stop motions, and the Goulding condenser were making Lancashire sit up and take notice; [84] and a Connecticut Yankee, Joseph Chessborough Dyer, was making a career in Manchester naturalizing American inventions. [85] The Metacomet Mill at Fall River may have been copied from a model mill in Oldham as late as 1846; [86] but the Lowell System, with its comprehensive processes, its rationalized layout, its high degree of mechanization and conservation of skills, and its large-scale production of a few, utility cloths by a semi-amateur female labor force, revealed to the world a peculiarly American genius for production; and the Boston Associates had evolved a corporate, capitalist organization of unrivalled power and effectiveness. As a result of these advances, New England had, by the Civil War, captured from Lancashire the domestic market for coarse cottons and consumed about a quarter of the cotton crop. In respect to this, the leading American industry in 1860, and the first modern industry to migrate across the Atlantic, the United States was ceasing to be complementary to Great Britain. Instead of being joint tributaries to an Atlantic Cotton Kingdom, the two countries had become competitors in manufacturing for the American market. An important westward shift of industry, a stage on the route from "colonial" to "metropolitan" status for the United States, had taken place.

British investors in American railways, even as late as the 1860's, were guided by promoters like Sir Morton Peto in the assumption that the American prosperity in which they expected to share should be agricultural. But the building of railways produced a boom, not only in the rolling mills of

Dowlais and Swansea, but in the infant iron trade of Pennsylvania, Maryland and Virginia. From 1846 onwards American rails rolled from American pig iron competed so successfully behind a protective tariff that in the late 1860's they were supplying the basic demand, British iron satisfying a merely marginal demand which fell away in slack times.[87] There is historic irony in the fact that not only British technicians, but British capital and railway iron in railways which married coal and iron fields, made a major contribution to the building of an American iron industry; and by 1860 this was on the way to depriving the British of their American market. With the colonization of an iron, and then a steel, industry on the western shores of the Atlantic, the United States had laid the foundations for a thorough-going industrialization which was to emancipate her from a "colonial" status and put an end to any semblance of complementarity between two regions of an Atlantic economy.

There is no need to labor the significance of 1860 as a terminal date for a major phase in Atlantic growth; but perhaps one may be permitted to end by emphasizing the importance of the Civil War in hurrying on an economic emancipation, which was only to be completed after the turn of the twentieth century with the reversal of the balance of payments. The election of Lincoln ended the long reign of King Cotton; it may also be said to have ended the most intense phase of an Atlantic economy. After the Civil War, with a national market and the rudiments of a national industry protected by a high tariff, with a new political unity and a marked nationalistic spirit, with the eclipse of the merchant by the manufacturer as the creative decision-taker who had the ear of government, the United States may be said to have bought out her British partner in the American enterprise. Thenceforward, for thirty years, many of the characteristics of an

Atlantic economy continued to determine economic growth; but the system was never again to attain the simple unity which characterized it during the first half of the nineteenth century.

2. British Political Radicals and the United States

THE Anglo-American connection transcended the facts of economic geography. Along the North Atlantic trade route there moved, not only goods, but people, the carriers of technical, philanthropic, religious and political ideas. The Atlantic economy supported a structure of social relations which bound together important elements in Britain and the United States.

The years between 1815 and the Crimean War were England's great Age of Reform, in many ways equivalent to America's Age of Jackson. In England, the political and social hierarchy of the eighteenth century was exposed to attack from a new social order demanding access to power and a re-vamping of institutions. The rebellious spirit which had led religious "Separatists" to New England persisted at home among those Independents, Baptists and Quakers who "dissented" from the official Church of England; and this spirit consorted well with that of growing numbers of tradesmen, manufacturers and artisans who chafed against the privileged order of land and status. These classes tended to be non-conformist, not merely in religion, but in a broader sense, outsiders, who refused to accept that state of life to which God had been pleased to call them, and who refused to conform to the traditional duties of an hierarchical order. Radical in politics and radical in religion, they forced the pace of social change.

At that time there was a marked contrast between the England of privilege, of aristocracy and land, of court, church, army, bar and bench, of learning and of great merchants, and the England of manufacturers, artisans and Dissenters who were outside the social pale. Moneyed men bought their way in, after the traditional fashion, as is evidenced by Pitt's unprecedented enlargement of the peerage; but the traditional order had hardly accommodated itself to the great social changes which accompanied the Industrial Revolution and the French Wars. For at least another generation, reformers, non-conformists in this broad sense, battered at the citadel of privilege, intent on dis-establishing, not only the Church of England, but all those institutions which supported a corporate, privileged order. In this great liberal program, English radicals were attempting to dismantle the "establishment," to reform the social order by instituting a quasi-republican form of government.

In their efforts, the reformers were acutely conscious of the United States. The trauma of uprooting was part of English folk experience; and non-conformists especially, whether Dissenters in religion, artisans by trade, or entrepreneurs in business, because of their outsider's attitude towards institutions, understood vicariously something of what it meant to become American. They recognized that what they were attempting in Britain had already been achieved in the United States. English radicals saw the America of the Age of Jackson as an incandescent example. For outsiders, the American republic was the hope of the world, just as for the insiders of the establishment, it was a subversive influence deeply to be feared.

In making this contrast between outsiders and insiders, one is aware of the dangers of over-simplifying the complex cross-currents of English political life. In particular, the use of the term "radical" to embrace working men, and middle-class manufacturers and traders, must not be allowed to obscure the fact that their interests often conflicted in domestic politics. When Disraeli described England as two nations, he referred simply to the rich and the poor, and the Chartist's enemy was as much the millocrat as the aristocrat. But the determining consideration for this study is the remarkable consonance in the way the outsiders, in the sense in which this term is here used, regarded the United States and used the American example for their own purposes. Not all radicals were pro-American, as the example of Charles Dickens, and others who will be mentioned, makes clear; nor were all Tories anti-American; but taking opinion towards America as a whole, the distinction makes a useful tool of analysis and contributes towards an understanding of what the United States meant to the England of that generation.

Orthodox English histories pay scant attention to the American theme; and, of course, the problems of English politics were domestic, and would be solved in a peculiarly English way. However, in the rhetoric of reform, the American example was powerful. As Dr. G. D. Lillibridge has well brought out, the contemporary speeches, newspapers, pamphlets, and journals which shaped radical opinion in the 1830's and forties were shot through with articulate references to the United States.[1] From the *Westminster Review* and *Edinburgh Review* to the *Poor Man's Guardian,* the *Working Man's Friend* and the *Northern Star,* American achievements, real or imaginary, figure prominently in all the successive phases and the different sectors of the radical attack. Although the power of popular ideas to influence events is difficult to assess, it is safe to say that the United States exerted a kind of lunar influence upon the tides of English politics in the Age of Reform.

There is little space to delineate the many ways in which

the American precept was drawn upon to drive home English argument. The radical attack itself was complex and comprised many disparate elements, often at odds with each other,
and sharing only a common hostility to the establishment.
Aristocratic Whigs and upper middle-class Utilitarians had
little in common with London workingmen; the artisans who
flocked to Chartist meetings had interests which conflicted
with those of the middle-class manufacturers who backed the
anti-corn law crusade; and if Dissent was a pervasive force,
from Methodist artisans to Unitarian and Quaker merchants
and professional people, there was a broad gulf between pious
evangelicals and atheistic free thinkers.[2]

However, from the agitation for the reform of Parliament
in the late twenties, the disillusion with constitutional reform
in the thirties, the Chartist and anti-corn law crusades of
the forties, to the mid-Victorian agitations for peace, education and laissez-faire, American precept, in different and
sometimes contradictory forms, was constantly deployed.

Agitators for the reform of Parliament and local government, both before the Reform Bill and even more explicitly
in the Six Points of the People's Charter, called attention to
the manhood suffrage, biennial elections, equal electoral dis-
tricts and the secret ballot in American States. Utilitarian
M. P.'s in the House of Commons, no less than working-class
editors, prescribed these American remedies for corrupt elections; for it was well known that in America elections were
as pure as the driven snow. It was argued that republican
institutions, with divided powers and limited, cheap government, were the remedy for concentrated power in the hands
of monarchy with attendant burdens in an expensive and corrupt court, and armed forces and a diplomatic service which
encouraged nationalism and war. The American boon of a
free, popular press was insistently dinned into the ears of

those who feared that the removal of the stamp tax on newspapers would lead to the spread of subversive, that is, democratic ideas. It was argued from American example that a
secular State in which all religious sects flourished with equal
freedom, but no sect was established, fostered religion and
morality; William Carpenter, editor of radical newspapers,
affirmed that "the most tolerant and equitable way to continue any peculiar class of Christians is, as in America, to let
it support itself: to protect all denominations from insult and
oppression, but to maintain none." [3] The absence in the
United States of the hereditary principle protecting the trans-
mission of power through a landed aristocracy was considered
a peculiar benefit of republican institutions. Benthamites, intent on reforming antiquated political and legal institutions,
praised American institutions for their efficiency and utility.
"The Americans," wrote the *Westminster Review*, "possess a
greater amount of happiness than the same numbers have
ever enjoyed before," [4] and Jeremy Bentham, himself, wrote
to President Jackson that he was "more of a United States
man than an Englishman." The manufacturing middle class
saw in American institutions an encouragement to enterprise
and prosperity, and a guarantee of that political and social
status which they were struggling to attain at home; and
Richard Cobden could affirm, "We believe the government of
the United States to be at this moment the best in the world;
but then the Americans are the best people." [5] The working
class attributed to republican institutions the high standard
of living of which they read in emigrants' letters; and the
Chartist journal, *The Charter*, could declaim, "The inhabitants of the United States are governed on the principles of
Chartism, the consequence of which is that all legislation is
bent towards the welfare of the many, and not of the few." [6]
This American rhetoric was not entirely based on hearsay.

The United States was so controversial a topic that authors, journalists and politicians took advantage of the convenience of Atlantic travel to visit that country to satisfy their curiosity and in the hope of writing a best seller about it. The result was a new kind of grand tour, not as respectable as to Florence and Rome, rather like the grand tour to the Soviet Union in the 1920's. The enormous spate of books on travel and manners in America which came from English publishers forms a well-known, indeed hackneyed, chapter in the history of Anglo-American relations.[7] Like most of their kind from that day to this, most British travellers on short visits saw what their personal prejudices led them to expect. Best known are those who, whether from deeply held conviction or irritation at a difference in manners, pronounced an unfavorable verdict; but for every Frances Trollope, Captain Basil Hall, or Charles Dickens who outraged sensitive American readers, there were others whose sympathies enabled them to take a more candid view of the New World. There was James Stuart, who had gone into voluntary exile after killing a Tory journalist in a duel; and James Silk Buckingham, ex-ship captain, journalist and Member of Parliament, whose reforming zeal ran the gamut from the abolition of flogging to free trade. There was the Rev. E. S. Abdy, a Cambridge don and an abolitionist. There was Harriet Martineau, political economist, that literary phenomenon of the age, whose ear trumpet recorded so much pertinent information about the United States; and there were numerous others such as Joseph Sturge, the Quaker, and George Combe, the phrenologist.[8] The writings of these authors, despite many different reservations about, and criticisms of, the United States, notably on the slavery issue, reveal a tolerance and detachment unusual among the insular English of that day. For they shared deeply felt reformist convictions. Their concern for human betterment took them beyond a narrow nationalistic patriotism into sympathy with the more liberal habits of mind of the American people. Their judgment of the young Republic was friendly and hopeful and they influenced English reformers.

But for many English people the vicarious experience of a tourist did not suffice. Among the tens of thousands of voyagers to America, in steerage and cabin, were a significant few who had chosen to settle in the new Republic for reasons of principle.

It is not easy to isolate the ideological element in migration; men's motives are mixed and, who knows, but that in the minds of the most materialistic a vague yearning for a "better life" did not subsume a hope for greater human dignity. The impulse of the rebel, of the outsider, to reject customary authority and to seek new opportunities in emigration remained powerful in the Atlantic world. This, the impulse which impelled the Scotch-Irish of Pennsylvania to seek the freedom of Kentucky, the Vermont farmer, the opportunities of the Western Reserve, or the radical, the anonymous wilderness for his experiment, was not confined to the western shores of the Atlantic. Many sorts of Englishmen—dispossessed farm laborers, dislocated craftsmen, unemployed factory workers, disgraced debtors and remittance men, persecuted freethinkers and agitators facing imprisonment, men frustrated by class barriers—looked upon America as a sort of black market world to which one could escape if one found adjustment to the demands of the customary community intolerable. And among these outsiders were a number of political radicals who rebelled at the institutions of unreformed Britain, and flocked to America to seek new opportunities, not so much for material advancement, as for a more rational form of citizenship. These men ranged from self-educated artisans, of the type of Francis Place, to well-to-do reformers of the type of Joseph Hume, and differed from their prototypes only in their determination to pursue their principles in the new Republic rather than in the reactionary England of Lord Eldon.

For such people America was an overpowering attraction. They responded to the promise of America's age of ferment, when horizons expanded so rapidly that an infinite progress in human betterment seemed possible; they saw eye to eye with those Americans who believed in the messianic vision of their country as a haven for the oppressed and a dedicated experiment in moral order. Such men thought of America, not as a foreign country, but as a projection across the Atlantic of their own aspirations, an experimental ground for those reforms which in Europe were Utopian but which in America seemed possible. They took fire at the idea of a State where men became citizens not by birth, as members of a tribe, but by choice, because they adhered to certain rational principles in social relations. In the afterglow of the Enlightenment, republican institutions seemed to be the key which would eliminate all the evils of civil society: class conflict, injustice, poverty, tyranny, nationalism, and war. There was something possessive and intimate in the regard which radical British emigrants had for the United States. This image of America was the secret of the great moral force which the United States exerted over the western world in the early nineteenth century.

It is difficult to generalize about British radical emigrants and their adjustment to America. Benthamites, Chartists, socialists, freethinkers, Dissenters, all saw different virtues in the country and made, or failed to make, different compromises with it. But for convenience they may be divided into two broad groups: firstly, the Utopians, those who looked to America to provide the negative boon of space and freedom to practice an idiosyncratic way of life away from the pressures of traditional conformity; and secondly, the activists, who committed themselves to American political life with the object of making it more nearly conform to the image of an ideal Republic which they had brought with them.

For the story of the Utopians one must begin in the years immediately after 1790 when the new Republic appeared to offer asylum to British sympathizers with the French Revolution. Two of the earliest to foresake England were the scientists Priestley and Cooper, the one a Unitarian minister, the other the atheist son of a Lancashire cotton manufacturer.[9] Priestley had seen his house set on fire and his laboratory destroyed by a mob which feared that his Unitarianism, his chemistry and his honorary French citizenship marked him as an infidel and a subversive. He settled with his family in a small community on the Susquehanna and set about proselytizing for his brand of Unitarianism. This is what he had to say about the United States:

The great excellence of this constitution consists in the simplicity of its object, which is the security of each individual in the enjoyment of his natural rights, without aiming at much positive advantage . . . The history of all the European governments shows that there is no wisdom in any government aiming at more than this. If it be empowered to . . . provide a religious creed for all the citizens, it may as well provide a philosophical one, and fix an unalterable mode of instruction in any of the arts of life: the consequences of which would be an effectual stop to all improvements. For every improvement, being suggested by individuals, would be opposed by the more ignorant and bigoted majority, educated in the old imperfect methods.[10]

The subsequent careers of these men, and especially that of Priestley in Pennsylvania are well known. Both Priestley and Cooper were in the end forced to come to terms with American society and to learn by bitter experience, at the time of the Alien and Sedition Acts, the practical limits of the republican ideal. The Susquehanna settlement did not long survive: but the idea remained attractive and at least one English family from the Priestley circle found its way ultimately to Robert Owen's New Harmony.[11] The example of this withdrawn community of choice English spirits in the American backwoods caught the imagination of that Romantic Age. Southey and Coleridge planned to establish their Pantisocracy adjacent to the Priestley colony.[12] A community of English professional people, organized by a Dr. C. B. Johnson, attempted a sort of Regency country idyll on the river after the Napoleonic Wars, growing English roses, lilacs and rhododendrons round the porch, dancing quadrilles on the carpeted cabin floor, and singing Mozart's operas to the accompaniment of the harp.[13]

The communitarian idea persisted, a jack-o'-lantern beckoning to restless English wayfarers from the American backwoods. Johnson was one of many who had been attracted to America by the beguiling pen of Morris Birkbeck. Birkbeck, brought up a Quaker, was a prosperous "improving" farmer in Surrey: he had been the first man to raise merino sheep in England and George Washington had once invited him to become his manager at Mount Vernon. After Waterloo he was unhappy about the prospects for farming because as a Dissenter he had to pay tithes to the Church of England, as a yeoman and a tenant farmer he had no vote, and as both Dissenter and yeoman he was an outsider, snubbed by the county society of Surrey. He joined forces with another family group, the Flowers and Fordhams, brewers of Hertford-

shire. These kinsmen were also Dissenters, either Quakers or
Unitarians; one uncle, Benjamin Flower, was a freethinking
pamphleteer and father of Eliza Flower, the evangelical hymn-
writer. Like Birkbeck, the Flowers were restive at the social
constrictions of county life. In 1817 members of all three
families emigrated to America. Rejecting Kentucky because
of slavery, they settled in Illinois. Here, hoping to transform
themselves from yeomen into squires, they developed a tract
of land as an English settlement, and imported scores of humbler fellow countrymen to people what became known as the
English Prairie. Within a few years it boasted a couple of
hundred immigrants. Birkbecks and Flowers on the frontier
tried to preserve the amenities of English civilized life,
founding a public library, building houses in brick and stone
in the style of the Regency cottage, laying out lawns, and attempting a more scientific farming than the backwoodsmen
around them knew.[14]

Although Morris Birkbeck preferred acting the part of a
gentleman farmer to grappling with the problems of frontier
cultivation, he became a man of some consequence in Illinois, and was the first President of the State Agricultural Society. He was also appointed Secretary of State; but his con-
firmation was refused by the legislature because of the part
he had played through his public letters and local influence
in blocking a move to have slavery recognized in the State.[15]
Birkbeck, who had visited at Monticello, was a fusion of
English Dissenting radical and romantic Jeffersonian. Despite advancing years and the sinking of his small fortune in
unrewarding Illinois, he never regretted the transplanting.
He rejoiced in the political climate of his adopted country,
and his writings about the United States are suffused with a
golden glow, like that of a painting by Catlin. Listen to him
addressing his fellow colonists on the Fourth of July 1822

when he had just become a citizen. His theme is patriotism and, following Montesquieu, he contrasts the advantages of "honour," the characteristic and meretricious quality of monarchy, concerned with public observances and leading to tyranny and injustice, with "virtue," that is, the virtue of the private man, which he regarded as characteristic of a republic:

It has been the policy of governments to cherish an overweening fondness for the peculiar habits, opinions and institutions of their own people and a contempt for those of other nations . . . This national spirit is dignified with the name of patriotism, but it is not the patriotism fitted for a republic. It is another of the props of arbitrary power, and, like the mimicry of virtue miscalled honour, is a mere counterfeit. Genuine patriotism is a ray of universal benevolence which beams upon every man as a brother. Beginning in the near charities of the domestic circle, it extends through family to neighbourhood—to country—to mankind.

This glorious principle, my fellow-citizens, is a sure bond of union in our great political family. Spread over so large a portion of the globe, from the State of Maine to the Gulf of Mexico and flourishing under a federal constitution, founded on this principle, it affords the most exhilarating view of human affairs that has ever been exhibited to the lover of his species.[16]

Birkbeck was drowned crossing the Wabash in 1824, clutching a big green umbrella, the symbol of his Englishry. Had he lived, he might have exercised an influence on the growth of his State at least as important as that of his younger British neighbor Robert Dale Owen in Indiana. As it was, his death, preceded by a personal estrangement with George Flower, led to the break up of the English community into its constituent homesteads, although the district kept a certain English *ambience*. But Birkbeck's influence was powerful in England. His persuasive *Notes on a Journey in*

America and *Letters from Illinois* excited English imaginations and, despite hostile polemics from Long Island by William Cobbett, who was hired by eastern land speculators to denounce the folly of settling in the interior, encouraged a number of similarly circumstanced families to emigrate.[17]

The colonies mentioned hitherto were the result, primarily, of a desire to escape from corrupt society into a quietist existence. We now come to two English communities which had the more positive aim of experimenting with what the sociologists would call "new forms of social action," one of which came to dominate the entire secular communitarian movement as it developed in the 1830's and forties.

In February 1826 George Flower travelled from the Birkbeck settlement to join Frances Wright's newly-founded emancipationist colony of Nashoba in Tennessee. Fanny Wright, it will be recalled, was a Scotswoman of means, passionate emotions and bluestocking intellect, who had sat at the feet of Jeremy Bentham in Highgate and had devotedly pursued Lafayette in France and round the United States in 1824–25. Enthusiastic about the United States, of which she published the inevitable traveler's account, and fired by the desire to emancipate the slaves, she returned to America late in 1825 to establish her little backwoods community in which a small slave force would work their passage to freedom by clearing and farming the land.[18] The tragi-comedy of Nashoba, which was doomed to failure, would be hardly more than a picturesque episode were it not a link in the chain which takes us from Birkbeck and Priestley to the Owens and New Harmony. Frances Wright owed the idea of Nashoba to the Owenite experiment which she had seen in its early stages at the Rappite colony of Harmony in Indiana across the river from the Birkbeck settlement; and it was to New Harmony that she repaired on the failure of her own venture.

It seems, in retrospect, inevitable that Robert Owen should have turned to the United States. The fabulous textile king, whose enlightened Scottish company town at New Lanark was a model for Lowell, having mastered the new force of industrial capitalism, had come to despair of making it serve a social purpose. It was characteristic of this impatient Welsh visionary that he should abandon the attempt to reform existing institutions, and should elect to show the world by example that a pilot model community, insulated from the corruptions of society, could solve the problem of industrial production in creative and socially responsible ways. Stimulated by Birkbeck and the Shakers, and confident from the wealth of his industrial success, he settled on a backwoods site for his experiment.

The New Harmony plan, first expounded before the uncomprehending but enthusiastic Houses of Congress in 1824, brought together many of the disparate elements in Anglo-American radical thought.[19] Owen's basic premise, inherited from the Enlightenment and shared by English radicals and Jeffersonian Americans, was the perfectability of Man in the right environment. The right environment involved the right institutions to encourage men to be social, and not predatory, animals; in emphasizing the utility of institutions against the sanctity of received tradition, Owen borrowed freely from his teacher Bentham. Among institutions Owen placed first education. He was among the first to see the importance not only of popular, but of creative, education which would foster individual talent and social co-operation. Education must also be secular; for men must be emancipated from the dogmas of religion. Linked with education was marriage, which should be a free contract between willing partners rather than the inhuman status decreed by property and religion in unregenerate society. As important as education was, of course, "the socializing of the means of production." For Owen, as for other radicals from Chartists to transcendentalists, industrial capitalism was a baleful force which would reduce men and women to predatory and servile beasts were it not controlled. Owen's solution, like Saint Simon's, lay in co-operative enterprise, at New Harmony in a combination of agriculture and handicrafts.

In much of this, Owen was at odds with other reformist opinion. His atheism alienated many Americans, even as it had shut the doors of London drawing rooms against him; and his socialism made no appeal to business men for whom laissez-faire for capitalist enterprise and supply and demand was becoming a dogma on both sides of the Atlantic. Yet this persuasive Welsh seer was well regarded even by those who held opposed beliefs; Alexander Campbell, the evangelist, described New Harmony as a "focus of enlightened atheism," and Jeremiah Thompson, our Quaker merchant of New York, was a friend of Owen and provided funds for the experiment. Opinion was still confused about the relation between religious conscience and free thought and about the nature of capitalism. In the wilderness, where co-operative effort was often necessary for survival, the communitarian idea seemed plausible; and in more metropolitan centres, radicals who were not socialists sympathized with the attempt to limit the operation of capital and to substitute for the indignity of capitalist and wage-slave, the independence of craftsman and husbandman.

The history of New Harmony is well known.[20] Owen's plan for a community in which property would be held in trust for its members, individuals would work according to their capacities, education would be designed to bring out those capacities and to inculcate a spirit of co-operative effort, the arts and rational debate would replace the dogmas and ritual of religion, all this proved too ambitious. Owen was away from Indiana for much of the time and his genius did not include a capacity for administration. Little attempt was made to secure a balanced community. A miscellany of European and American intellectuals, half-baked enthusiasts, drifters and hangers-on swamped the industrious farmers and artisans who should have formed the bulk of the population. Intellectual debate gave way to bickering and repeated secessions. Within three years the community had broken down into its constituent settlements which, though preserving a distinctive style, reverted to old unregenerate habits. Without Owen's personality, and with his fortune squandered, the Old Adam reappeared like a dryad from the backwoods and Utopia was defeated. Had Owen proved a great leader, the community might have persisted on a handicraft basis, like the Shaker or Oneida communities, until a national economy should sweep it into oblivion.

But its influence persisted. According to Professor Dorfman, Robert Owen was the greatest source of inspiration for early American labor thought.[21] New Harmony influenced the communitarian movement of the thirties and forties and inspired several direct imitators. During its brief life the experiment attracted a remarkable group of individuals to the Indiana backwoods: advanced social thinkers like Josiah Warren, Frances Wright, Robert Dale Owen, and the Scot A. J. Macdonald, the first historian of the communitarian movement;[22] educational pioneers like the Pestalozzians Neef, d'Arusmont, and Madame Fretageot; scientists like Say, the entomologist, Troost, the geologist, and Lesueur, the botanist, who were to contribute to an American natural science and, by attracting the younger Owens to science, helped make one a geologist and the other one of the founders of the Smithsonian Institution. New Harmony's influence was perhaps richest in education and science; and for this Owen's partner, William Maclure, was largely responsible. This wealthy Scots importer from Philadelphia, geologist, and president of the American Geological Society, shipped the famous "boat-load of knowledge" down the Ohio, provided the driving force behind New Harmony's educational experiments, and endowed township libraries in Indiana to which one local authority attributes the high literary fecundity of the State.[23] In this, and also in Robert Dale Owen's reform of the state marriage and divorce laws which made Indiana the nineteenth century Nevada, the influence of New Harmony may be discerned in the tradition of the State.

New Harmony was the high point of Utopian radicalism in Anglo-American relations. Apart from minor influences like that of the Englishman Charles Lane who financed and shared in Bronson Alcott's "Fruitlands" venture or the British recruits for Etienne Cabet's Icarian venture to Texas, interest now shifts to the second strain, mentioned earlier, the activists, concerned not with an insulated experiment but with reforming existing American institutions, a more hopeful proposition than reforming those of Britain.[24]

After New Harmony, Owen, himself, returned to unregenerate Britain to promote new panaceas: co-operation and a Grand National Trades Union to tame the savagery of the capitalists. His son Robert Dale and Frances Wright, after her flamboyant tour of lectures on co-operation, free thought, feminism, and free love, together in 1828 moved their *New Harmony Gazette* to New York with the object of taking command of the workingmen's parties in that city. The activity of these two ardent spirits, through their newspaper, renamed the *Free Inquirer,* their Hall of Science, their public lectures, and speeches, marks the start of intervention by British radicals in workingmen's politics on the eastern sea-

board. It was not a happy intervention. It was often ineffective, obscure, and transient. Where they succeeded in giving
a lead it was usually false and the very association of English
radicals gave to the workingmen's movement the taint of a
foreign-inspired conspiracy against the United States. But for
the Atlantic connection this English influence is significant.

Historians have normally held the view that the rise of
organized labor in America, both in its trade union and its
political aspects, largely parallels that of Britain. Both originated in late eighteenth century trade societies and struggles
against the common law of conspiracy; the first union of
trades in Britain was organized in Manchester in 1826, the
first in the United States, in Philadelphia, in 1827; the first
national trade union in England, Owen's Grand National, in
1834, the first in the United States in the same year. Both are
found more among the older crafts than in the new factories;
both display the same mixture of political and industrial
aims. Although direct correspondence between the early
British and American unions has yet to be unearthed, the
rhetoric of early American labor journalism, with its wealth
of references to the plight of the British worker and the need
to prevent his fate overtaking the American, would suggest
close transatlantic contact. If the American movement contributed "boss" to labor slang, the nomenclature, even the
term "trade union," and methods and objectives like the ten-
hour day, were predominantly British. The American movement may, in its early stages, be fairly treated as an extension
of the British, taking its cue from situations which were already critical and chronic in the older country, but were
coming to be recognized as dangerous for the new.[25]
One reason for this intimacy was the fact that among the
workingmen of Philadelphia, New York, New England, and

minor centers were a significant number of British origin. Among factory workers, as was indicated in Chapter I, textile operatives were particularly obstreperous. Scottish carpet weavers organized a prominent strike at Thompsonville, Connecticut, in 1833 to protest against wages cut below the rate which had enticed them across the Atlantic.[26] The Lancashire cotton spinners of Fall River took the lead in forming the New England Mechanics Association of 1844; through their Fall River Mechanics Association they struck repeatedly for higher wages and a ten-hour day, and they pioneered consumers' co-operatives like that of their Rochdale cousins.[27] The first miners' union was formed by an English miner among the British coal mining communities of Pennsylvania, and the first generation of union leaders were almost exclusively English, Welsh, and Scots, many of whom had emigrated after the Chartist debacle of 1848 and the collapse of the Scottish Miners' Association of 1856.[28] The activity of these migrants is difficult to plot; but here and there a British-born artisan raises his head above anonymity, like John Samuel, the Welsh glass blower who in 1836 was engaged in a general strike and later organized the glass workers in Philadelphia, or the Scots dyer, Robert Macfarlane, who edited a mechanics' newspaper and organized a Mechanics' Mutual Protection Society with branches in New York State and the West.[29] Although these men may hardly be considered transatlantic carriers of political ideas, their background in, and uprooting from, the industrial metropolis gave them a superior knowledge of the trends of the times and an aptitude for agitation.

A few, however, were more articulate and contributed to the growing corpus of labor literature. William Heighton, the shoemaker whom Mr. Louis H. Arky has discovered for us, emigrated as a youth from Northamptonshire to Phila-

delphia where in 1827 he organized the pioneer Mechanics'
Union of Trade Associations.[30] In the previous year, this
"unlettered mechanic" as he styled himself, had published
an influential address which provided the Philadelphia trade
societies with a crude economic theory to justify their demands. The starting point of Heighton, and of the other
early American pamphleteers like Skidmore and Byllesby,
was a crude form of labor theory of value, derived from the
Ricardians, usually at second hand through such writers as
Robert Owen, Thomas Spence, the agrarian netmaker of
Newcastle, John Gray, the Scottish economist, or John Francis Bray, who, after writing *Labour's Wrongs and Labour's
Remedy* in Leeds, himself migrated to the United States and
lived out an obscure existence in Michigan.[31] The American
literature is largely derivatory. In ideas, as well as leadership,
the early labor agitators depended heavily on importations.

The artisans of Philadelphia and New York were beginning, in their unlettered way, to formulate a theory and program of industrial action to protect them from the increasing
bouts of unemployment, wage cutting, and rising prices. But,
like their Chartist fellows in Britain, they were too unsure of
their ground not to be beguiled by the possibility of better-
ing themselves by political means, by using the new weapon
of the vote to obtain social reforms. It was at this moment of
uncertainty, during the depression of 1828–29, that Robert
Dale Owen and Frances Wright arrived in New York with
a mission to provide the workingman with the benefits of
intellectual leadership.

The intervention of intellectual radicals immensely confused the workingmen of New York. Owen, Frances Wright,
and their satellites, used their considerable eloquence to
direct the "Workies" not only to politics, but, with apoca-

lyptic urgency, towards the immediate and catastrophic reform of all American institutions in the direction of what
they regarded as enlightened republicanism. This meant the
entire range of nostrums which Benthamism, Owenism,
Nashoba, and New Harmony had manufactured. Audiences
were treated to empassioned disquisitions on an equal, rational and state-maintained boarding school education run
on the best Pestalozzian principles; on the evils of organized
religion and the beneficence of free thought; and, if this
were not enough, on the importance of free relations between the sexes. The Free Inquirers, like the Garrisonians
after them in another sphere, believed that reform must be
universal; no half measure could be tolerated. It was no wonder that humble artisans and shopkeepers recoiled from such
heady notions into the arms of Tammany Hall, and shunned
the strange European figures who were bringing down on
their heads the outraged hostility of the "respectable element."

Frances Wright and the younger Owen sojourned only a
short while in New York. By 1832 the workingmen's parties
had been largely captured by the regular political machines
and workingmen turned again to union activities. Frances
Wright left the city for marriage and France in 1830, Owen
for Indiana in 1833, having retreated from much of his father's socialism, and on the verge of his true career as a reformist politician in his adopted State. However, British immigrant radicals continued to drift in and out of New York,
Brooklyn and Philadelphia, forming a loose, semi-bohemian
society which continued to give radical ideas a nasty foreign
name and which must have been embarrassing to those respectable merchant families of the British community. By
means of obscure, strident, and opinionated newspapers and
cranky little societies they kept alive the principles of free

inquiry. They were never altogether out of touch with politics and they preserved an Anglo-American link.

In New York George Houston, who was a friend of the English free-thinker Richard Carlile and had been jailed in Newgate on a charge of blasphemy (for translating d'Holbach's *Ecce Homo*), edited *The Minerva* and in 1827 founded *The Correspondent*. This was a free thought and anti-clerical paper, emphasizing "a diffusion of correct principles, which alone form the basis of morals and happiness," and "the paramount importance of the laws of nature and the dignity of Reason." This paper, until the New Harmonists arrived, was the principle free thought organ in New York, and agnostic societies were founded in Philadelphia and elsewhere.[32] In the thirties and forties, a group of kindred souls published a succession of little newspapers, *The Man, The Beacon,* and *The Diamond* and ran a Moral and Philosophical Society for the General Diffusion of Useful Knowledge.[33] These organs harmonized on a series of familiar barber shop chords: free thought and anticlericalism; Tom Paine and the Rights of Man; free trade; Bentham and the utility of institutions; Robert Owen and the rights of labor; Frances Wright and rights for women; popular education; science over superstition; hydropathy and phrenology. They promoted books like G. H. Evans' edition of Paine and Strauss' *Life of Jesus* and gave prominence to news from Britain and articles and poems by "advanced" English writers like Thomas Campbell and Mary Howitt. To John Quincy Adams, these publications "indicate the pertinacity with which this little atheistic club pursue their will-of-the-wisp over the low, swampy, lands of Christendom." [34]

Like similar groups in England they organized, at the Knickerbocker Hall next the Park Theatre, annual dinners to celebrate the anniversary of Thomas Paine, with a long succession of toasts, such as:

The People of the United States, as a Nation the offspring of common sense; the disciples of the Age of Reason: may they preserve their sovereignty from the deceits of a priesthood; and the assumptions of an aristocracy.

(drunk to the tune of *Yankee Doodle*)

or:

Education: Liberal in principle; universal in extent; the handmade of Free Inquiry; may it distinguish this mighty and rising nation, and be distinguished by it.

(to the tune of *Hail Columbia*)

or:

The Liberals of the present age: rivulets in a mighty stream which in its course will destroy ignorance, bigotry, and superstition.

(to the tune of *The Liberty Tree*)[35]

and they erected by subscription a monument to Paine in New Rochelle. One of their speakers was Benjamin Offen, an English shoemaker and self-educated lecturer on free thought and religion; but their chief spokesman was Gilbert Vale, an interesting man and a lively journalist.[36] Vale, who had come from England at about the age of thirty in the 1820's, was a man of some education (he taught navigation for a living) who had been intended for the ministry but had become a passionate freethinker. He wrote a life of Paine and kept up an unending flow of invective, exhortation, and instruction in *The Beacon* which he edited and financed. He was a character. "Take a man," said Walt Whitman, "take all sentiment, poetry, philosophy out of him: that is Vaill: a hard nut," but "a valuable, rare old man to know." [37]

There was also Thomas Brothers, a Warwickshire hatter

who emigrated to the United States in 1825 under the influence of the ideas of Thomas Paine. He practiced his trade for several years on South Front Street in Philadelphia. In the stormy times of the early 1830's, however, a number of experiences—with worthless banknotes, antislavery riots, the burning of the Pennsylvania (antislavery) Hall, the cruelties of the much vaunted Pennsylvania prison system, the corruption of democratic politics—brought disillusion with American institutions and prompted him to a brief career in labor politics. In the summer of 1835 he intervened in the agitation for a ten-hour day and published yet another abortive radical newssheet, *The Radical Reformer,* which brought him into contact with Philadelphia labor leaders and New York Radicals.[38] He would be of no more than local antiquarian interest except that his disillusion with a banker-ridden Republic, racily expressed in his paper, became so bitter that he turned his back altogether on the United States and in 1839 returned to Britain where he published a searing denunciation of his temporarily adopted country entitled: "The United States of North America as They Are: Not as They are Generally Described; being a cure for Radicalism." [39] With this English hatter, that belief in the therapy of republican institutions, which obsessed most British radicals, turned to despair and apostasy.

The year in which Thomas Brothers took his return passage to Old England saw the westward Atlantic crossing of the first of a new group of stragglers from British radical politics who were to add a piquant flavour to the bohemian stew of the seaboard cities: the Chartist exiles. The Chartist admiration for American institutions went so far that the *Southern Star* published a memorial requesting the President of the United States to intervene on behalf of Chartists after the Monmouth and northern uprisings of 1839–40.[40] To seek safety in the United States was the first instinct of Chartist agitators on the run from the police. Many, George Holyoake who was one of them, believed hundreds, chose this escape route. They were a miscellaneous crew. For some, America was no more than an asylum. Feargus O'Connor paid but a brief visit; and Peter M'Douall, member of the Committee of the National Charter Association, and leader of the Manchester Plug Plot of 1842, returned when it was safe to do so.[41] Others sank back into the obscurity from which they had briefly emerged. Some reacted strongly against the United States, like the Scots waiter in Utica whose disillusion with democracy had begun with a rascally runner met on landing at New York; [42] or G. J. Harney, editor of *Northern Star*, who despite a radical reception committee, remained sourly sceptical of the United States:

A social revolution in America is a necessary complement to the political revolution of '76. Should no such revolution or reformation, come to pass, the future of America cannot fail to be a copy of Europe at the present time—the community divided into two great classes: a horde of brigands monopolizing all the advantages of society, and a multitude of landless, profit-ridden slaves, deprived of even the name of citizens.[43]

He finally returned home. Still others put radical agitation behind them and, responding to American environment, embarked on entirely new careers. M. M. Trumbull became a successful Chicago lawyer although long afterwards old beliefs made him defy public opinion by demanding clemency for the Haymarket anarchists.[44] Allen Pinkerton, the son of a Glasgow police sergeant, reverted to family type and became the freebooting detective commander.[45] W. H. Bellamy made his living as a successful actor of old men's parts; [46] just as W. J. Linton, sometime editor of *The English Republican* and a voluntary emigrant after the Civil War, was to make his way as a wood engraver of importance.[47] But there were some whose crusading zeal did not evaporate in the salty air of the Atlantic, and who found their way, sometimes with previous introductions, to radical meetings where their long harangues were treated with the respect due to soldiers fresh from the field of battle. Of these, three stand out.

John Campbell was an Irish weaver in Manchester who had been secretary of the National Charter Association. On his release from prison in 1842 he emigrated to Philadelphia where he became well known as a bookseller and publisher of law books at Sixth and Chestnut. He retained violently radical views, took part in radical societies, became Horace Greeley's Philadelphia labor correspondent, and in 1848 wrote a *Theory of Equality*, dedicated to the French revolutionaries of that year. The argument of this, which begins with Rousseau and Paine and proceeds to the advocacy of common land ownership, national workshops, and labor exchange notes, is reminiscent of Josiah Warren, although according to its author it derives from the Chartist leader, Bronterre O'Brien.[48]

More influential than Campbell was John Cluer, who arrived in the United States with fraternal messages from English workingmen in 1844. A Lancashire textile operative, he immediately went to work to apply his experience as an agitator among the New England cotton spinners. He took a leading part in the campaign of the New England Association for a ten-hour day, which he proposed to achieve by calling a convention of operatives and manufacturers, petitioning the legislature and then, if all failed, by calling a general strike. His career was marred by the discovery that, like other emigrants, he was a bigamist; but he continued to be an active advocate of land reform and a temperance speaker.[49]

The most important of the three was another Irish-born Chartist, Thomas Ainge Devyr. After an obscure, journalistic career in the Dickensian half-world of London, this wild, passionate agitator was drawn into the Chartist movement in Newcastle, where in 1839 he helped to arm the Northumberland workers with pikes and homemade grenades. When the hue and cry was raised he escaped to Liverpool where, narrowly avoiding some home office agents whom he overheard discussing him in a pub, he was rowed out to the *Independence* as she sailed for America a jump ahead of his pursuers. Arriving in New York in 1840 with sixpence in his pocket he went to work for a Democratic newspaper in Brooklyn during the Van Buren campaign. Quickly read out of the local Democratic Party for his wild views, he established his own printing shop and radical newssheet, the *Williamsburg Democrat* and plunged vociferously into immigrant radical politics in New York.[50]

Like O'Connor, O'Brien and other Chartist leaders of the forties, Devyr's background was not industrial but Irish and agrarian; and this determined his whole attitude to radical politics. The United States originally attracted him because, as he had written in Chartist days:

the foundation wrong of all [is] monopoly of the soil . . . "That will surely be broken up with every other wrong as soon as we get a government by Universal Suffrage" so they said, but whether rightly or not we shall see by the lesson taught in America where universal suffrage exists. [For,] the sole cause of American freedom is, that the energies of her people and her political influence are not under the influence of landlords. So long as land can be easily purchased by the in-coming emigrant, all shall go well; . . . but farewell to the plenty and happiness and freedom of the NEW WORLD and welcome the rampant tyranny, the slavery and wretchedness of the OLD, [if the landlords obtain control].[51]

With this conviction and warning, he quickly turned his attention to a nearby political struggle which seemed to threaten the liberties of Americans. This was the antirent movement on the feudal estates of the Van Rensselaers up the Hudson River. In June 1842 he appeared in person on this new battlefield, and signed a pact with the Helderberg farmers, "they to help me free the public lands to actual settlers only, I to aid them in their local war." [52] For the next three years, in Brooklyn and up the Hudson where he briefly edited the *Albany Freeholder*, he agitated against the monstrous tyranny of feudal landlords in the New World. The story, well told by Henry Christman, ended in defeat and, as usual with Devyr, recrimination.[53] But the episode illustrates an important strain of Anglo-American radicalism: the demand for free access to the land.

Throughout the tracts and manifestoes of many of the radicals hitherto mentioned there runs the reiterated theme of land monopoly. In an age before industrial capitalism had become accepted as the dominant economic order—for even in England the state of the crops and the price of corn were still the most important indices of economic life—the thinking of radicals was predominantly agrarian. At a time when English, Irish and even American tenants were being evicted, Ricardian ideas about rent, and the existence of a class of aristocratic landlords, led to a preoccupation with the ownership of the soil. In England, the middle classes rallied to the slogan of "free trade in land" and working class opinion went further. Radicals from Cobbett to the later Chartists were anticapitalist, not in the sense of Engels and Marx, who accepted industrialism and wished to take it over, but in the sense of being totally hostile to the ugly industrial order as revealed in the dark satanic mills and cottages of Manchester and Leeds. This dislocated generation yearned to return to an older order of yeoman and craftsmen. In these circumstances, the cry, "Back to the land," had a magic appeal; and when, in 1843, the more advanced Chartists, despairing of political reform and faced by competition from the Anti-Corn Law League, sought a practical plan on which to rebuild the Charter Association, they turned to the land. Feargus O'Connor, starting, like Devyr, from Irish experience, proposed that landlords should be compelled to turn over their acres to cottage tenants and workingmen should co-operate to buy holdings on which they could settle, and which would carry the coveted forty-shilling freehold franchise.

In the foreground of their thinking was the example of the United States. English Chartists, like their American counterparts, had their own version of the safety valve theory. For them republican institutions rested upon the existence of land which small men could easily acquire and farm. They did not advocate emigration for English workers. On the contrary, O'Connor was hostile to emigration plans like those of the potters mentioned in Chapter I; Englishmen should settle at home if the reform was to effect a social revolution. They were also aware of the limits of the safety valve theory, and the danger that with grasping landlords and thrusting industrialists, America might go the way of Britain. However, during the forties, the *Northern Star* and other Chartist papers reprinted lengthy extracts from the *Working Man's Advocate, Young America, The Radical,* and the *Daily Sentinel* which kept them informed of the thinking of kindred spirits in America in these matters. And in 1844 they were especially heartened by the news that a group of reformers in New York had launched a movement for the distribution of free land to settlers which, along with their own scheme, promised to strike twin blows at propertied tyranny in the Atlantic world.[54]

For the American land reformers one must go back to a more famous English emigrant. George Henry Evans, born of middleclass country stock in Herefordshire, came to the United States in 1820 at the age of fourteen with his father and brother. He was apprenticed to a printer in Ithaca. Bookish, and of some education, he found his way to New York where, on Thompson Street, he opened the inevitable printing shop, and in 1829 started to publish the *Working Man's Advocate*. During those stirring times for working men, Evans belonged to the Free Inquirers, and he was a particular admirer of Frances Wright. Attracted by the communitarian idea, he sent his brother Frederick to inspect existing communities, with the unexpected result that the latter became converted to the Shaker faith and ended his life as a leading Elder. George, however, remained in New York until the break-up of the workingmen's party when, in 1837, he retired to a farm in New Jersey. Here, reflecting on the failure of the Workies, he came to the conclusion that the Owenite program, however "suited to the meridian of England," [55] was irrelevant to America, and that the solution to the specific problem of the mechanic lay in the land. The provenance of Evan's thought is obscure. But whether the seed lay in Britain, or, as he later asserted, in native American conditions, George Henry Evans based his argument on Skidmore, the American interpreter of Spence, Paine, whose works he edited, and Jefferson.[56] Man had a natural right to the land and the remedy for the evils afflicting American society lay in the free access of genuine cultivators to the public domain. In 1844 Evans returned to New York a tireless advocate of a program which, under the slogan "Vote Yourself a Farm," stipulated the freedom of public lands to settlers, exemption of homesteads from seizure for debt, and the limitation of the amount of land any one person might acquire. He started anew the *Working Man's Advocate* (later re-christened *Young America*), and at a meeting of New York radicals at John Windt's printing shop he launched the National Reform Association.[57] Of the six charter members who met at Windt's shop that day three, Evans himself, Thomas Devyr, fresh from his exploits in Rensselaer County, and James A. Pyne, a picture-frame maker, were British immigrants.[58]

This is no place to embark on the events which unfolded from that meeting. The National Reform Association was the spearhead of a campaign which culminated in the Homestead Act. This is part of American national tradition; and takes us far beyond Atlantic history. But I hope that this Cook's tour, which has taken us to well-known shrines and murky back streets where we have met a few celebrities and many obscure people, may have helped us to envisage the multitude of particular moments in which radically-minded Englishmen and Americans communicated with each other. It is only by pursuing innumerable contacts among individuals that one may understand the true influence of ideas. I hope, also, that this sketch may have revealed a common Atlantic outlook which had some bearing on political events.

In dwelling on that aspect of an Atlantic outlook which concerns the British in America, I hope it will not be thought I have indulged in the chauvinism which is the special pitfall of ethnically-biased historians of migration. The dominant fact of Anglo-American radicalism was the very existence of the United States: the example of Republican institutions in action. This was the lodestar which determined the field of force. But the facts of trade, migration, the frontier, the Atlantic economy, determined that the impact of America on England should be more indirect, if more pervasive, than the limited, more specific, more direct influence of Britain upon the United States. For ideas are carried by individuals; and because of the immense attraction exerted by the New World, the traffic in individuals across the Atlantic was predominantly westwards.

Looking back on the thirty years after the Treaty of Ghent —Harriet Martineau's *Thirty Years Peace*—the character and limits of Anglo-American radicalism come more clearly into focus.

Firstly, in so far as there is an Atlantic world of radicals, it belongs to what I have called outsiders. In a sense all Americans were outsiders: for their republican principles had forever set them apart from the corporate, customary societies of the Old World. This is why it is sometimes difficult to isolate the radical spirit in the United States, and also why in Britain the very existence of the Republic was a standing challenge to the establishment. On the other hand, the outsiders in Britain, radicals, non-conformists, were, by the very nature of the society, more easily identifiable, and more specifically connected with the United States. In both countries radicalism was concerned with the attack on the establishment. In the United States, the outer defences of this fortress had been breached at the Revolution; but for Jacksonian radicals the inner bastions—the Greek temple on Chestnut Street, the manor of Rensselaerwyck, the mansions of Beacon Hill—had still to be stormed. In Britain, the fight against privilege had hardly begun, and for the radical ranks, the success of the American revolutionaries had acted like a successful cavalry charge on the flank.

Secondly, radicalism was concerned with the problem of property. Not all radicals saw eye to eye on this and there were many radically-minded people who saw good, not evil, even in industrial capitalism. The radicalism of such people was limited to the attack on privilege and in the 1840's in England they turned to the crusade to abolish the Corn Laws. These will be dealt with in the last chapter. The radicals we have been chiefly concerned with here, working class and intellectual, were hostile to the concentration of property and especially industrial capitalism. American radicals in a country where industrialism had not yet taken hold feared and fought it, and English radicals were particularly attracted to a country where the existence of unlimited land and a less advanced economy held out the hope that it might be scotched altogether. American workingmen and Chartists alike began with the naive assumption that by acquiring the vote they could curb the power of bankers, landlords, and capitalists to oppress working people. Disillusion led to more radical diagnosis. The Utopian few despaired of reform and followed Owen in advocating ideal communities insulated from the world, and these looked especially to sites in America. Most mechanics turned to industrial action, to unions, and to strikes. Others, hankering still after social reform, concentrated on the land question. For Chartists, beset by the problems of an already industrialized country, such a remedy proved to be a will-o'-the-wisp which led them into the sands of 1848. But in the less advanced United States, with a frontier of unsettled land, the National Reformers started a movement which was to influence national policy. Out of all the elements seething in the radical crucible, it is significant that the ultimate, hard residue should have been a land policy.

Thirdly, Anglo-American radicalism transcended national patriotism. Revolutionary sentiment about the brotherhood of man persisted in this Anglo-American world where ethnic affinities and ease of communication encouraged extra-national loyalties. And especially for those Englishmen who emigrated, the overriding loyalty was not to country, but to the betterment of man. For such people, the American Republic was not just another country, but a rational experiment in human government in which all could share who had the will to believe; and they moved from one country to the other caring little for the kind of patriotism which stems from tribal consciousness. Joseph Priestley, according to his biographer: "never clearly grasped that America and England were two distinct nations . . . America was the England, on a large and predominant scale, of Lansdowne House and the philosophers of Birmingham and the Americans were their countrymen." [59]

Robert Owen casually took out first papers of American citizenship in 1824, and then five years later as casually abandoned them. And Frances Wright, in defence of Paine's Americanism against nativist views, passionately protested:

> For what is it to be American? Is it to have drawn the first breath in Maine, in Pennsylvania, in Florida, or in Missouri? Pshaw! . . . Hence with such paltry, pettifogging . . . calculations of nativities! *They* are American who, having complied with the constitutional regulations of the United States . . . wed the principles of America's Declaration to their hearts and render the duties of American citizens practically in their lives.[60]

The extreme views of English radicals about American citizenship clearly define the limited nature of an Atlantic community of ideas in relation to American society and politics.

Fourthly, the sentiments just quoted, as indeed most of those used in this chapter, also clearly define the limited nature of an Atlantic community of ideas in relation to British society and politics. The British who felt most at home in the

climate of Anglo-American radicalism were those who started
from a belief in natural rights. By no means all did so. The
Lockean tradition which provided Americans with an all
but universally held corpus of beliefs about society, did not
hold quite the same ascendency in British political thought
or habit, even among radicals. The limited nature of this
common ground is well illustrated by the American connections of Benthamism. In applying the test of utility rather
than sanctified tradition to British institutions in the interest
of the greatest happiness of the greatest number, the Utilitarians were attracted by the United States. Bentham, it will
be remembered, considered himself "more a United States
man than an Englishman," and British emigrants like
Frances Wright, the Owens, or Gilbert Vale had studied
Bentham. Bentham also had several American disciples:
Richard Hildreth, whose translation of Dumont's redaction of
the *Theory of Legislation* introduced that work to the British public; Edward Livingston who drafted the Louisiana
legal code; John Neal of Portland, William Beach Lawrence
of Columbia University. Benthamite assumptions were im-
plicit in many of the social reforms advocated in both countries: in the attack on the clergy, in the rationalism of free
thought; in the emphasis on "science"; in the program for a
rational education and a more rational marriage contract.
But Benthamism had little direct influence in the United
States. Here the battle against privilege and obscurantism
seemed won and there seemed little need for it as an intellectual system since its practical applications were accepted as
common sense. But there were more important reasons. The
British Benthamites, upper-middle-class professional men for
the most part, wanted to reform the establishment, not abolish it. They believed in strong government by the enlight-

ened few in the interests of the greatest number, not in limited government and diffused rights. And this belief rested upon an assumption in their political thought which contrasted fundamentally with that normally held by Americans. As Professor Paul Palmer of Princeton has pointed out, their philosophic premise, that "all rights are the creatures of government," was basically at odds with that of natural rights.[61] In this respect Benthamism was capable of adjustment to more traditional views of English political liberties and of being woven into the corpus of beliefs of a reformed establishment. It is not accidental that Benthamism is the most persistent strain of English radicalism. For English radicals did not, of course, succeed in republicanizing Britain. American solutions were discovered to be irrelevant to the genius of English society. In the seventies and eighties English reform was to move far from the common ground of Anglo-American radicalism of the thirties and forties. That common ground, in so far as we have seen it in this chapter to exist, was the result of particular circumstances and of special misconceptions about the common nature of American and English society. In the event, the basic stuff of two national cultures proved too strong to allow a common political tradition to develop.

I have, in fact, as you will have noticed, had to go into the highways and byways to find my Anglo-American contacts in the field of political radicalism. The comparatively minor character of many of the actors in this chapter is sufficient demonstration of the tenuousness of the idea of an Atlantic connection in this respect. Yet the community of ideas has importance, if not in itself, in its relation to another aspect of Anglo-American radicalism, that of the humanitarians, the philanthropists, whose beliefs were paradoxically so different and yet whose actions allied them, at least in England, with the political radicals. Here the community of ideas across the Atlantic is close and important. It is the subject of the next chapter.

3. The Anglo-American World of Humanitarian Endeavor

THE starting point of the last chapter was the British non-conformist. It will be remembered that this term was used in a broad sense to include those groups in British society who by temperament and circumstance were set apart from the established order and who wished to reform that establishment in the interests of a more individual, and rational, morality. These were the groups who felt a special kinship with the United States. The last chapter examined the American relations of one section of British non-conformity, the political radicals; this turns attention to the other element, the religious radicals; the sixth tries to show that the two groups are by no means entirely separate, and that together they form a distinct Anglo-American connection.

The starting point of this chapter is the Dissenters, the members of the great Non-conformist sects who, as a result of being shut away from the power and patronage of the established order had, by the close of the eighteenth century, created their own distinctive world, with its chapels, academies, journals, and its great interlocking family and mercantile connections. It was a world which had close relations with the United States.[1] In 1793 an Anglican bishop was of the opinion that "the principles of a Nonconformist in religion and a republican in politics are inseparably united," [2] and, in Southey's view "the American War made the Dissenters feel once more as a political party in the state. New England was more the country of their hearts than the England wherein they had been born and bred." [3] The *Edinburgh Review* was more specific when in 1838 it reviewed Harriet Martineau's *Retrospect of Western Travel*, published after her return from the United States. Miss Martineau was, it will be remembered, a daughter of the great Norwich circle of Dissenting families which included the Gurneys, Smiths, Taylors, and Aldersons; and her brother James became the leading divine in the English Unitarian church.

She belongs to that party in England, religious and political, which, ever since the days of Priestley, has kept up a peculiar connection with one of the most important portions of American society. The very strongholds of that party in England—Liverpool and Manchester—are allied by close mercantile ties to Boston and New York; and the alliance of mind is closer still. The party of which we speak does not count a very numerous following in either country; but it is peculiarly distinguished by its high intellectual cultivation and by a certain degree of exclusive pride with which that cultivation is attended. In England its tenets approach to a tempered republicanism; in America, it is looked upon as rather aristocratically inclined. But this is a difference which the opposite circumstances of the two countries naturally seem to produce; for, in England, intellectual superiority, wherever it does not bow in willing subjection to the existing oligarchy of birth and wealth, always has a tendency to train off from it and form a commonwealth apart; in America, a high degree of education is looked on as a sort of title of nobility, and regarded with some jealousy by the multitude. Affinity of opinion has produced between members of these parties on each side of the Atlantic, a sort of cousinship and similarity of manner and tone of thought, not to be met with between any other classes in the several countries. The slight peculiarities, both of habit and mind which appear to characterise

well educated Americans of the Eastern States are more nearly
to be matched among the higher classes of dissenters in the great
provincial towns of England than anywhere else; and an English
Unitarian, especially if connected by family and acquaintance
with the select people of that sect in his own country, is pretty sure
of meeting in America not only with the kind and hospitable
reception which all travellers with good recommendations can
procure, but with a sort of family greeting.[4]

The Anglo-American connection to which the *Edinburgh
Review* particularly referred consisted of those families, mercantile and professional, educated and often intermarried,
who had come to Unitarianism, in England either as lapsed
Anglicans or as descendants of the old Presbyterians, in America from the Congregational and Episcopal Churches.[5] In the
England of Priestley's generation, as we have seen, the Unitarians were identified, not only with infidelity but with
Jacobinism; and thenceforward the sect was coloured by
those liberal attitudes towards faith and society, which were
to appear in deeper shades in the career of Harriet Martineau
herself.[6] It is hardly surprising, therefore, that English Unitarians should have sympathized with the American revolutionaries and should look towards the United States for
asylum during the reaction against the French Revolution,
and thenceforward as an example of enlightened, republican
institutions. The Priestley colony on the Susquehanna was
not the only English Unitarian community-in-exile in the
United States. The first permanent Unitarian Church in
Philadelphia was founded in 1797 as a result of Priestley's
lectures among a group of young English Unitarian emigrants; [7] and the thinking of English Unitarians powerfully
influenced Church congregations in New England and New
York in their search for a more liberal creed and liturgy. The
Rev. William Hazlitt, father of the essayist, visited Boston

and gave decisive advice to Freeman and his flock at King's Chapel; the writings of Lindsey and Priestley provided the frame of reference within which American Episcopalians and Congregationalists followed their more advanced English brethren towards the full Unitarian position.[8] Thenceforward, after the capture of Harvard College and Boston, the New England Unitarians advanced independently and so rapidly that by the 1830's the writings of William Ellery Channing and Theodore Parker were setting the pace for James Martineau and his English Unitarian flock.[9] Although advanced in theology, American Unitarians remained more conservative than their English co-religionists in social values; for these Boston merchant princes and their clerical allies had already achieved their revolution, and they did not have the same impulse towards social reform which continued to characterize some of the English Unitarians. But by and large English and American Unitarians shared a common set of values, powerfully influencing Atlantic opinion. Well-to-do and commercially connected, they habitually crossed the Atlantic in both directions, a traffic made easy by letters of introduction to Boston families and that informal consular service provided by the Rathbones and other Liverpool merchants in the American trade.[10]

The *Edinburgh Review*'s description would equally have applied to the Society of Friends. The Quakers on both sides of the Atlantic formed a community, even more closely connected than the Unitarian, of intermarried, largely mercantile, families fenced off from the outer world by their particular beliefs and discipline. The American Revolution had hardly disturbed the intimate relations between London and Philadelphia Yearly Meetings. Minutes were diligently exchanged; members were "released" for ministry in the other country; and important missions, like those of Stephen Grellet of Philadelphia to Britain and of Joseph Sturge, or J. J. Gurney to the United States, and the services of Quaker merchants often connected with the American trade, like the Thompsons in New York and James Cropper in Liverpool, were elements of a communications system as efficient, in its sphere, as the official diplomatic service.[11] When the London Meeting for Sufferings wished to stop the import of rum into the South Sea Islands, Philadelphia Meeting duly passed on their minutes to Moses Brown, the Providence merchant, who had dealings in those parts.[12] London Yearly Meeting contributed to the support of the poorer American meetings, to the establishment of new meetings in the West, to the building of schools and the provision of Bibles. When evangelicalism tinged English Quaker doctrine, it was London's representative, J. J. Gurney, who influenced orthodox American Quakerism in the same direction, and thereby helped to perpetuate the Hicksite schism; and when the Indiana Yearly Meeting revolted against orthodox policy towards the slavery controversy, a mission was sent from London in 1845 in vain to heal the breach.[13] At the center of every aspect of humanitarian endeavor there was to be found a small body of Quaker philanthropists in England led by such men as William Allen and Joseph Sturge, providing organization and finance; and although in the United States Quaker influence was more diffuse and less dynamic, it was probably not less important.

But the Unitarians and the Friends, though probably the most influential sects, were small in numbers. Other, more popular denominations, although without the cohesion of Friends and Unitarians, preserved and strengthened their transatlantic links after the American Revolution. Presbyterians, Congregationalists, Methodists, Baptists, and Episcopalians, all established fraternal relations with their British co-religionists, corresponding on matters of doctrine and organization and exchanging delegates. Typical of such exchanges, for the years 1835–36 alone, were the visits to Britain of John Codman and Heman Humphrey from the New England Congregational Church and of the British Congregationalists Andrew Reed and James Matheson to the United States, the delegacy of Wilbur Fisk from the General Conference of the Methodist Episcopal Church of America to the Wesleyan Methodist Conference of Great Britain and that of F. A. Cox and J. Hoby from the British Baptists to the American Baptist General Convention.[14] The American Methodists, who benefited greatly from the dis-establishment of the Church of England, and the Episcopalians, who suffered by it, re-defined their apostolic relations with their parent English bodies. The sects of the richer country contributed funds to their American denominationalists. Bishop Chase of Ohio, the Rev. Nathaniel Wheaton, and Bishop Hobart of New York, raised funds among prominent Anglicans like Admiral Gambier and Lord Kenyon to found the General Theological Seminary and the colleges of Kenyon, and Washington (later Trinity), Connecticut.[15] Later, in 1844, this flow of funds was counter-balanced by funds raised among American Presbyterians for the endowment of the new Free Church of Scotland.[16] Controversies like the Hicksite schism among Friends, the Free Church schism in Scotland, the quarrels over lay leadership involving the Methodist Protestant Church in America, and the Wesleyan Methodist Connection in England, and the conflict between evangelical and high church wings of the Episcopal Church, had repercussions and parallels in both countries. And as will be seen, the slavery controversy caused complex divisions in most denominations.

These sectarian connections were greatly strengthened and

affected, at the opening of our period, by new winds of faith and doctrine which stirred most churches and deepened the transatlantic influence of religion. That "Protestant Counter-Reformation," the Evangelical Revival, set its stamp on a whole Anglo-American generation, and is of special importance to the Atlantic connection.

In the first place, as far as England was concerned, it particularly affected those classes which had the greatest affinity with the United States. It is true that its most powerful antecedent was the Wesleyan revival of sixty years before, that perhaps its most characteristic expression was the Methodism of the generation after John Wesley's death, and that the Wesleyan Methodists, having remained so long within the Established Church, supported an authoritarian church discipline and continued to claim intimate relations with the Church of England. However, although the Wesleyan Connection remained in a sense a bridge between the Established Church and Dissent, increasingly in the nineteenth century the spirit of Methodism, appealing as it did especially to the rising artisan and trading classes whose social connections were with Dissent, must be regarded as Non-conformist in character.[17] It is also the case that at the outset evangelicalism's most powerful directing force was that group of aristocratic politicians, bankers and Anglican clerics of Clapham and Cambridge who burrowed from within the Church Establishment. But the Clapham sect were denounced by High Anglican Tories as Methodists, only one remove from Jacobins, and the evangelical party remained a small, though highly influential body, within the Church of England.[18] Though connected with what we have called "the establishment," evangelicalism was essentially rebellious and disruptive, and brought considerable strength to the mobilized forces of Dissent. For, in the words of an Anglican historian, the evangelicals "cared little for the Church or for the State as a Divine institution. Their business was with personal salvation," with individual as opposed to corporate religion.[19] They thus encouraged a non-denominational temper, represented by the Evangelical Alliance of 1846 which united Anglicans and Non-conformists, and they were prepared to work with all Churches on both sides of the Atlantic in moral reform. In fact, the Evangelical Revival achieved its most notable successes among the commercial, manufacturing, and artisan classes, the growth of which, especially in the new industrial towns, was the chief phenomenon of the age; and its spirit probably exerted its widest social influence among the Non-conformist sects which, although representing a fifth of the population, in the opinion of Professor Halévy "equalled if they did not exceed the Anglicans who practiced their religion." [20]

In the second place, the Evangelical Revival, though owing much to the pietistic writings of Germans like Arndt and Francke and the humanitarian practices of such centres as Halle and of the Moravians, may be treated in its later aspects, as an Anglo-American movement.[21] It appeared about the same time in England and America and evangelists in each country powerfully affected each other. The movement may be said to have originated with the ministries of the two Englishmen John Wesley and George Whitefield. But the moment was propitious, for perhaps different reasons, on both sides of the Atlantic. Wesley reaped his most fruitful harvest in the English, and Whitefield in the American, vineyard; and if England produced the organizing genius, New England produced the movement's most formidable theologian. As a Congregationalist scholar has pointed out, its origins cannot be divorced from the Great Awakening which took place in Connecticut in the years 1736–40. "We have to go back," writes the Rev. E. A. Payne, "not to the Epworth Rectory where John Wesley was born on June 28th, 1703, but to a home in Connecticut, New England where, on October 5th of that same year, Jonathan Edwards saw the light." According to this authority, Edwards was "the decisive influence . . . on the new life which carried the Church out to distant continents." Edwards exerted a powerful hold over Whitefield, whose convictions were "cradled and strengthened" in America in 1740 and, through Whitefield and by his own writings and correspondence, Edwards influenced a number of important British divines, including John Erskine of Edinburgh, the Baptists Robert Hall, Andrew Fuller and William Carey, founders of the Baptist Missionary Society, and Thomas Chalmers, the founder of the Free Church of Scotland. For "classical Calvinism had within itself the essenitally evangelistic impulse." [22] It was significantly a New England divine who provided the most powerful argument pointing the way from total depravity and predestination to conversion and salvation. Jonathan Edwards and New England successors, like Emmons and Hopkins, provided British evangelicais with such useful ammunition that Newman complained of "American dissenting divinity" in English vicarages.[23]

This interplay may be traced through the later course of the movement. The most powerful impulses which transformed orthodox religious habit in the Atlantic world radiated from Clapham and Cambridge, England. At the time when Britain was on the threshold of world maritime power, the outlook of her evangelicals, like that of her merchants, was expansive, all-embracing and oriented overseas—did not Charles Simeon claim India to be his diocese?—towards all continents including North America. By contrast, the American temper remained provincial and derivative, taking its lead from the ex-mother country, in spirit—William Wilberforce's *Practical View* ran through an edition a year in the United States from 1800 to 1826—and, as will be seen, in organization. Yet America contributed her own intense revivalistic practices. Whitefield's early success had come during those long journeys through the American back-country from Georgia to Massachusetts at the time of the Great Awakening and the peculiar quality of the backwoods revival eventually touched the mean streets of England.[24] Wesley may have started the practice of circuit riding and open-air preaching from farm wagons; the Welsh may have early had their own form of holy rolling and the jerks, but the techniques both of camp meeting and urban crusade were imported into England from the burnt-over district of western New York and the Broadway Tabernacle.[25] After each of the great conflagrations of 1801, 1826, and 1857, the spiritual arsonists of America—Lorenzo Dow, Charles Finney, James Caughey, William Taylor, Phoebe Palmer, and others—crossed the Atlantic to kindle the dry tinder of English industrial towns. The visit to England of the American Methodist Lorenzo Dow inspired the camp meeting at Mow, in Chesire, in 1807 which prompted the carpenter Hugh Bourne to break away from the Wesleyan Connection to found the Primitive Methodist Church.[26] In 1844 Charles Finney inspired the young London shop assistant, George Williams, to start the Young Men's Christian Association which soon, in turn, found its way across the Atlantic to the United States; and it was from the Chicago YMCA that Dwight Moody began the evangelist mission which was to take him so often to Britain. That frontier phenomenon, the camp meeting, was not without influence in the metropolis.

Religious "enthusiasts" in Britain looked especially towards the United States. Some, like the Methodist William
Arthur, crossed the Atlantic to evangelize America.[27] Others,
like the political radicals, went further. An exotic few, from
Mother Ann Lee and her Manchester Shakers in the 1770's
and the Mormon recruits from English towns and villages in
the 1840's and fifties to the aristocratic Laurence Oliphant
at the mystical community of Brocton in 1867, migrated to
America in search of seclusion for spiritual experiment.[28]
American utopianism had a messianic strain, and "come-
outers" on both sides of the Atlantic were convinced that the
United States held out a special hope for spiritual progress.

Anxious Seat, Shaker dance, and Mormon trek were for
ignorant and inarticulate folk; but they represent the exotic
fringe of a religious movement which profoundly influenced
Atlantic opinion. Highmindedness, piety, and zeal united the
Churches of America with the interlocking connection of Dissent and evangelicalism in Britain in the common object
of spiritual regeneration and moral reform. "Unite Britain
and America in energetic and resolved co-operation for the
world's salvation," wrote two Congregationalist delegates
from Britain to the United States in 1836, "and the world is
saved." [29] They spoke for a generation of earnest souls whose
brisk traffic across the Atlantic was concerned with nothing
less than world salvation. And it was a generation which
thought in extra-national terms; as Professor Spiller has written of the Americans among them who went to Britain:

[None] could be said to be either pro-British or anti-British.
Their minds were coloured by religious rather than patriotic
sympathies, they recognised the bonds of race and of human
brotherhood to the exclusion of national antipathies and of political antagonism. They went to England to visit those who spoke

and believed as they did and they were welcomed as brothers in the faith.[30]

We are dealing with a genuine Atlantic community.

This co-operation quickly went further than Church doctrine and administration. Since the essence of evangelicalism was the saving of souls, it can hardly be conceived apart from the missionary movement which grew up within it. Here, as one would expect with a movement of world horizons, the initiative came from the metropolitan country. The missionary activities of the British evangelicals were minutely copied in New York, New Haven, and Hartford. Wilberforce's first preoccupation, the Society for the Suppression of Vice, was reproduced in New York by the society of the same name in 1802. Robert Raikes' Sunday School was copied by the Philadelphia First Day Society of 1790 and later by the American Sunday School Union, while, independently, Samuel Slater had carried in his head to Rhode Island the model not merely of his erstwhile employer's spinning frame, but of his Belper Sunday school.[31] Hannah More's Religious Tract Society, founded in 1799 was followed within four years by the Massachusetts Society for the Promotion of Christian Knowledge, and later (1814) the New England, and then (1823) the American Tract Society. The great British overseas missionary societies, and especially the non-denominational London Missionary Society (1795) which was working in Canada before the end of the century, and the (Anglican) Church Missionary Society were quickly paralleled by American missions to the Indians and ultimately by the Board of Home Missions.[32] In 1816 at the prompting of, and with funds from, the Church Missionary Society there was established the first American overseas mission, the Domestic and Foreign Missionary Society of the American Episcopal Church. In 1804 the concern

of British evangelicals at the lack of Bibles, especially among
the Welsh and the Canadian Indians, led to the formation of
the British and Foreign Bible Society. Four years later the
Philadelphia Bible Society was founded to remedy a similar dearth in the American back-country, and it was followed
in the next few years by the formation of some sixty-two
other Bible societies in America, culminating in the American Bible Society of 1816. These were supplied by the British society with Bibles and stereotype plates and by funds
which at the close of 1817 amounted to over three thousand
pounds.[33] A similar service was provided by English Quakers.
The poverty of the world in the matter of the Holy Writ
overrode all considerations of patriotism. During the War of
1812 the British and Foreign Bible Society supplied Bibles
to American prisoners of war in Dartmoor and the American
Bible societies subscribed to buy the cargoes of British Bibles
captured by American privateers and sent them on their way
to the Canadian Indians.[34]

It was only a step from the souls of Indians and Africans
to Christian souls maimed by physical and social circumstance. The acid of evangelicalism gave a sharp etching to
the benevolence of the Enlightenment. Penal reform owed
much to the legal and utilitarian outlook of Bentham and
Romilly; but it began in the 1770's with a Dissenting Sheriff
of Bedford, Robert Howard, and caught public imagination
in 1817 with the evangelical ministry to the prisoners of
Newgate, by the Quakers Elizabeth Fry (sister of J. J. Gurney) and William Allen. This, too, was an Anglo-American
as well as a French movement. Stephen Grellet, who had a
Quakerly concern for prisoners in his native Philadelphia,
is said to have been instrumental in arousing Elizabeth Fry's
interest in London; [35] and the penitentiaries at Philadelphia,
Auburn, and Sing Sing, with their rival and so-called im-

proved systems, were objects of earnest investigation in the 1830's by European reformers.[36] The idea of visiting America was first suggested to Harriet Martineau by a philanthropist's saying: "Whatever else may be true about Americans, it is certain that they have got at principles of justice and mercy in the treatment of the least happy classes of society which we may be glad to learn from them. I wish you would go and see what they are." [37] She made a point of visiting American prisons and it is symbolic that she crossed the Atlantic with Dr. Julius, the Prussian prison reformer, just as her fellow reporter, E. S. Abdy, had crossed a few months previously with William Crawford, investigating prisons for the British government, and both followed in the wake of a more famous pair, de Tocqueville and Beaumont, engaged on a similar errand.[38] Reform in the treatment of the insane owed most to the example of the English Quaker, Samuel Tuke, whose description of his Retreat near York provided a text for the establishment of a Quaker retreat near Philadelphia in 1817 and other asylums in New York and Massachusetts which, in turn, were the basis for Dorothea Dix's campaign of the 1840's.[39]

These ardent and impatient men and women, in their war of the spirit, were not content with local successes. Only an eccentric fringe may have thought in terms of the Millennium; but many hoped for large, strategic victories in the Atlantic campaign of moral reform. Philanthropic radicals attacked simultaneously on several broad fronts. The first spate of activity, beginning in the last decade of the eighteenth century, was concerned with the saving of souls through the agency of Bibles, tracts and home and foreign missions; the second, beginning in the years of peace following on 1815, was concerned especially with three evils which appeared to that Anglo-American generation to be the most corrosive to the human spirit: drink, war, and slavery.

Before dealing with this three-pronged attack, a word must be said about the methods of organization. These campaigns were elaborately mounted. Doing good by modest example was not sufficient, especially in the cases of war and slavery. It was necessary to awaken the conscience of nations. New and ingenious techniques of agitation were invented which revolutionized the machinery for mobilizing public opinion and ultimately, as will be seen, the practice of politics itself. In America, agitation had broken the power of the British establishment at the Revolution, and now in England what might be properly called a public opinion was beginning to influence the narrowly-based politics of the landed gentry. In both countries the techniques for forming public opinion were powerfully influenced by the Evangelical Revival. The preacher who called sinners to repentence became the agitator who demanded immediate and sweeping moral reforms. The agitator was a characteristic early Victorian figure. As Daniel O'Connell said, "I am a practiced agitator and I know that you can never succeed in the most just cause without agitating the public mind until you have a sufficient moral force by means of public opinion." [40] The agitator was a new and important phenomenon: an orator, capable of moving vast audiences to laughter, tears, and moral indignation; a fundamentalist, concerned with ends, not means, with principle, not practice. We have already met the agitator among the political radicals; and in the gallery of Anglo-American agitators, alongside such figures as Frances Wright, Thomas Devyr, and John Cluer, must be placed philanthropic radicals like John Bartholomew Gough in temperance, William Lloyd Garrison, and George Thompson in antislavery, Elihu Burritt in the peace movement and, above all, that past master of the art, Wendell Phillips, whose energies extended to antislavery, temperance, feminism, and labor reform. It is perhaps significant that most of these mentioned were Americans; for it was in that populistic democracy that the agitator's powers were most fully developed. As Phillips put it, "the agitator's purpose is to throw the gravest questions upon the conscience of the masses because they are the ultimate governors in a republic." [41] However, the agitator became a powerful force in moral reform on both sides of the Atlantic.

If the Americans excelled as agitators, the British genius lay in organization. Agitation involved propaganda. It was only a step from riding the preacher's circuit and distributing Bibles and Cheap Repository Tracts to holding public meetings, raising funds, pamphleteering, and placarding; only another step and, behold, there had come into being that great force which has become the very stuff of Atlantic politics: the voluntary association, or, if you like, the pressure group, devoted to a single, urgent reform. The British antislavery leaders were pioneers in developing methods which were to become standard for other reforms in Britain and, to a modified extent, in the United States. Local, voluntary societies up and down the country organized processions, public meetings, and lectures, raised funds, distributed pamphlets, signed pledges, memorialized the Queen, the President, and State Governors, and petitioned Parliament and Congress. These local societies were linked together to support a national organization with "anniversaries" or conventions and a central office with salaried agitators and officials to promote new auxiliary societies, conduct campaigns and exert pressure on government.[42] The British headquarters of philanthropic radicalism was Exeter Hall in the Strand, built in 1831; its American counterparts were the Marlboro

Chapel, Boston, built in 1838, and the ill-fated Pennsylvania Hall, Philadelphia, built and burnt in the same year. Although these methods were peculiarly well adapted to mobilize the power of the politically under-represented middle class in Britain, they were a major means of agitation in both countries; and if the men who directed the campaigns—in Britain such representative men as Joseph Sturge, Thomas Fowell Buxton, William Allen, J. J. Gurney, George Thompson, James Silk Buckingham, in America, the Tappan brothers, William Jay, Gerrit Smith, Samuel May, Henry C. Smith, W. L. Garrison, James Birney, Joshua Leavitt, Elihu Burritt, Frederick Douglass—if these men were something of a stage army, appearing in different uniforms in different scenes, their influence upon philanthropic opinion was profound.[43] The finishing touches were given to this organization when, in the 1830's, not only were the British methods adopted in America but the two countries became linked in a single Atlantic communications system. Correspondence, pamphlets, journals, "Friendly Addresses," and memorials were exchanged and reprinted, delegates voyaged back and forth, and by 1840, the first of a series of "international," that is to say, largely Anglo-American, conventions trumpeted to the world the unison of philanthropic endeavor in the Atlantic world.

An early and logical extension of missionary work was the crusade against strong drink. The temperance movement was a peculiarly Anglo-American contribution to the reform of morals. The pervasiveness of evangelicalism is shown in the fact that efforts to combat drunkenness became manifest at about the same time in relation both to the urban masses of Britain and the largely rural population of the United States. However, its origins and chief leadership were American.

Cheap spirits and gruelling conditions in isolated settlements combined to make drunkenness a special problem of the frontier. The first temperance society was organized in 1808 among the lumberjacks of the little frontier town of Moreau, New York, and there came to be a strong concentration of such societies in that "burnt-over" district of western New York which Gilbert H. Barnes and Wilbur R. Cross have shown to have been a weather-breeder of the evangelical climate.[44] But western New Yorkers were largely transplanted New Englanders and the leadership in the crusade to put down strong drink was provided by the east and especially by the evangelical empire of New England. The Massachusetts Society for the Suppression of Intemperance, founded in 1811, marks the start of twenty years of mushroom growth in temperance societies which, in 1831, were estimated at four thousand in number.[45] The American Society for the Promotion of Temperance was founded in 1826 and in 1833 (the year of the American Anti-Slavery Society) a multitude of local societies were federated into an American Temperance Union.

This American example prompted a sister movement in Britain. John Dunlop of Glasgow was impressed by the temperate habits of the wine-drinking French; but he drew upon American facts and experience for lectures in 1828 which led to the formation of the first temperance societies in Scotland.[46] This example together with the "Six Sermons" of Lyman Beecher of the Massachusetts society, spurred Henry Forbes, a Bradford merchant, to organise a society in his own city in 1830 which was quickly followed in the same year by the formation of some thirty other societies in the industrial north with a reputed membership of ten thousand.[47]

This colonization was rapidly annexed, in a way which was becoming standard, to the evangelical empire; and it owed not a little to the experience of Bible, tract, and especially, antislavery, societies. In 1831 temperance leaders united at the new headquarters of philanthropy in Exeter Hall as the British and Foreign Temperance Society, and within a year fifty-five auxiliary societies had been affiliated and nearly one hundred thousand pamphlets issued.[48]

Nathaniel Hewitt of the American Society for the Promotion of Temperance was present at the inaugural meeting, and from the start relations between the British and American societies were close. American delegates like Hewitt and E. C. Delaven took a lead in drafting policy. Vast quantities of American pamphlets were distributed, special attention being paid to warning intending emigrants of the special dangers of drink in the United States.[49] American speakers, from E. C. Delaven in the thirties to the spellbinder John B. Gough in the fifties, commanded large, enthusiastic audiences.[50] English visitors to the United States like Joseph Sturge concerned themselves with the progress of temperance in America and J. S. Buckingham earned large sums there as a temperance lecturer between 1837–39.[51] This co-operation reached a climax in 1846 with the holding in London of a World Temperance Convention, along the lines of the Antislavery Conventions of 1840 and 1843. This Convention, with its twenty-five American delegates and with Lyman Beecher as vice-president, was an Anglo-American jamboree.[52]

British and American crusades were rent by similar dissensions over policy. As will also be seen in the case of the peace and antislavery movements, there was conflict between "gradualists" and radicals. Many of the earliest temperance advocates, concerned only with the evils of dram drinking, were averse from taking a stand on beer or wine. But evangelicals, impatient, dogmatic, and fundamentalist, and reformers with experience of drunkards, came to demand a pledge of total abstinence for all true believers. The term "teetotal" was probably coined in England in 1833 at a meeting of the society formed by the famous "Seven Men of Preston," led by Joseph Livesey;[53] four years later the teetotalers withdrew from the national society to form a new British and Foreign Society for the Suppression of Intemperance on a basis of total abstinence.[54] In the same year, E. C. Delaven and other root-and-branch men introduced a thoroughgoing teetotal pledge to the American Temperance Union which caused heated controversy throughout the movement in the United States.[55] A similar conflict in the British society between "long" and "short" pledges, was eventually solved in 1839 by the adoption of the American pledge after a debate, in which Delaven and other Americans participated.[56] The two movements had other common characteristics. The temperance hotels which Joseph Sturge so much admired in New England, were paralleled on a more modest scale in Britain;[57] a concern for youth promoted Bands of Hope in England and Cold Water Armies in America; and although Britain developed no separate Washingtonian movement, there was also a shift from the prevention of drunkenness to the cure of the drunkard. As with the peace and antislavery movements, temperance moved from moral exortation to political action: and here again the Americans took the lead. The prohibition of the sale of intoxicants by law in the State of Maine in 1851 was a new spur to temperance efforts in Britain. Two years later the United Kingdom Alliance was formed in Manchester to lobby Parliament for a similar measure; and Neal Dow, the Quaker merchant of Portland who was responsible for the Maine

Law, was brought over in 1857 to promote it.[58] The contrast between the failure of British temperance enthusiasts to do more than impose gradually more stringent regulations on the sale of intoxicants, and the persistent, and ultimately triumphant prohibition movement in the United States illustrates a difference in national temperament. But within those limits the temperance movement must be regarded as Anglo-American in its inspiration. Although the earnest deliberations of the temperance crusaders make dreary reading now, their influence transcended its immediate object. In Britain especially, temperance, appealing as it did to the chapel-going, manufacturing middle class, became an important element in the moral force which was mid-Victorian radicalism.

During the World Temperance Convention in 1846 at a soirée held at the Freemason's Tavern, Joseph Sturge persuaded some sixty delegates to sign a new pledge, not to temperance, but to peace.[59] The peace movement also had Anglo-American origins and drew strength from the Atlantic climate of reform. The English-speaking peoples seemed destined by Providence to lead the world on a crusade to eliminate war. Despite the serious diplomatic friction between the United States and Britain in the 1830's and forties, reformers and philanthropists came to see special possibilities for peace across the Atlantic. Here at least, between two countries with complementary interests and achievements in political and social reform, it should be possible to make progress with techniques for the peaceful settlement of international disputes. For the first time one hears the heartfelt belief, commonplace now, but novel then, that if the common people of the two countries could know each other there would be no war. Albert Prentice, the Anti-Corn Law Leaguer, voiced these popular sentiments in 1848. Speculating on the possibilities for Atlantic travel of a new paddle wheeler, he wrote:

. . . With a reduction of one half of the time and one half of the expense I do think that there could be no more wars between the two countries. The citizens of the United States do not dislike Englishmen individually; . . . Their dislike is to John Bull—the traditional, big, bullying, boroughmongering and monopolist John Bull . . . And *we* do not dislike the citizens of the United States. . . . Our dislike is to Jonathan—bragging, annexing and repudiating Jonathan. The individual likings will become the national in proportion to the greater intercourse of the individuals of both nations. Give us then the quick and cheap steamboat. The paddle wheel is the emblem of civilization and peace. Why may it not be regarded as one of the means, in the hand of God, to hasten that happy time when men shall beat their swords into [plowshares] and their spears into pruning hooks and shall learn the art of war no more.[60]

It was thirty years before the peace pledge and these sentiments by a Manchester traveler that the Anglo-American peace movement had its origins. After the turmoils of Napoleonic and American Wars, a few evangelicals had been seized with the revolutionary desire to limit and, if possible, abolish war. They hoped by the new opinion-forming techniques to mobilize a national opinion strong enough to hold in check the warlike tendencies of what would now be called "power diplomacy." An English group, meeting at the London house of the Quaker, William Allen, had discussed the idea of forming a peace society as early as June 1814; but it was the news of the forming of such a society in Massachusetts in 1815, together with a telling tract by an American, Noah Worcester's *Solemn Review of the Custom of War,* which spurred them in June 1816 to organise the London Peace Society.[61]

Co-operation between the London and the American societies which came together in 1828 as the American Peace
Society, remained so close that it is impossible to think of
the two organizations except as part of a single movement.
The English peace men held special hopes for the cause of
peace in the American Republic. An early report of the London Peace Society ran as follows:

Our transatlantic friends are moving forward in their most
honourable course with unabated zeal and ardour; and removed
as they are from the scenes of bloodshed, your Committee hope
that peace will find a safe and serene asylum in the land which
was peopled by our sires and which we would fain regard as
possessed by our brethren.[62]

And many radicals would have subscribed to the belief of an
English peace advocate that there was something in American
institutions "more favourable to the progress of pacific principles" than in British institutions. The Americans, for their
part looked up to the London Society for its zeal, resources,
and organizing capacity.[63]

British and American peace advocates evolved common
policies and experienced similar controversies. The London
Peace Society, dominated by the Friends, took its stand on
the principle that "all war whether offensive or defensive is
upon Christian principles utterly indefensible." [64] Such a
thoroughgoing pacifism went far beyond the more limited
objectives of "practical" advocates of international arbitration; but tact and forebearance, especially on the part of
such men as Henry Richard and Richard Cobden, and a temperamental preference for compromise, enabled the two
groups to work together. In the United States, on the other
hand, a more extreme conflict between conservatives who
justified defensive war and out-and-out pacifists was only set-

tled in 1837 when the American Peace Society adopted a formula in line with that of the London society.[65] Even this was not enough for the *outré* temperaments of Henry C. Wright and William Lloyd Garrison who developed a doctrine of non-resistance, the logic of which implied the complete breakdown of civil government. These radicals hived off to form the New England Non-Resistance Society in 1838.[66] There was another temperamental difference between British and Americans. The Americans favoured especially William Ladd's ambitious goal of a Court and Congress of Nations; on the other hand, although the London Peace Society had sent Thomas Clarkson to the Congress of Aix-La-Chapelle in 1818 to lobby for such a scheme, the more pragmatic and cautious British were on the whole sceptical of what they came to call "The American Plan," and preferred to concentrate upon the more limited objective of arbitration.[67]

The crusade developed a crescendo of activity between 1837 and 1852. Meetings and lectures were held, auxiliaries formed, and funds raised; pamphlets were distributed by the hundred thousand, journals were published, like the *Herald of Peace* (English) and the *Advocate of Peace* (American), and there was a continual exchange of correspondence, literature, and visits across the Atlantic. In 1843 following the pattern set by the antislavery movement, the British and American Societies came together in London in a World Peace Convention which, with Sturge, Lewis Tappan, and Amasa Walker as vice-presidents, was predominently an Anglo-American affair, and the model for the more truly international peace conventions of Brussels, Paris, Frankfort, and London which followed from it between 1848 and 1851.

This activity was quickened by diplomatic friction between the two Governments. The succession of crises from the *Caroline* and Arostook affairs of 1838 to the Oregon question of 1846 presented a direct challenge to this Anglo-American movement. During the Oregon crisis "Olive Leaves" were broadcast through the press in both countries, and there originated in Birmingham, England, a system of "Friendly Addresses" between pairs of British and American towns like Manchester and New York, Boston and Boston, and between British and American working men, manufacturers and merchants. This "People's Diplomacy" achieved spectacular publicity.[68]

The organizing genius behind this propaganda was Elihu Burritt, "the learned blacksmith" of Worcester, Massachusetts, who left his native shores to promote the cause in Britain in 1846 at the height of the Oregon crisis. Walking with knapsack and staff on a country road towards Worcester, England, that summer, he conceived the idea of a great League of Universal Brotherhood, bound by a pledge of peace; and at the little village of Pershore he collected pledges from twenty country people, the first members of a rapidly growing association which by 1847 boasted thirty thousand pledged members in England and America.[69] The League pursued a broad program. In addition to organizing Friendly Addresses between Britain and France and distributing Olive Leaves, it promoted an ocean penny post to encourage international understanding among common people, and, like the temperance movement, assisted emigrants bound for the United States. Its advocacy of an English boycott of American slave-grown cotton took the movement into antislavery territory and illustrates the tendency of all reform movements in the late 1840's to impinge on each other in a broadening objective of "universal reform." [70]

The League of Universal Brotherhood, with its peace pledge, was the high point of moral insurgency against war.

But like all such pledges of good intentions, there was danger of a relapse. Something more than moral exhortation was necessary if the public concern which the League had aroused was to be made effective. The peace movement, like the temperance and antislavery movements was drawn irresistibly from moral exhortation to political action.

"The American Plan" for a Congress of Nations did not get beyond pious resolutions at peace conventions; but the idea of writing arbitration clauses into treaties looked more promising. The original idea was the work of an American, Judge William Jay, son of the negotiator of Jay's Treaty and a president of the American Peace Society. His proposals were seen by Joseph Sturge during his visit to the United States in 1841; [71] and on Sturge's initiative were adopted by the American and London Peace Societies and, in 1843, by the London Peace Convention.[72] These arbitration proposals, along with resolutions dealing with the munitions trade, were subsequently reaffirmed at the international peace congresses, beginning with that at Brussels in 1848. In 1849, Richard Cobden, at the prompting of Joseph Sturge and after a barrage of agitation by the League of Universal Brotherhood and the Peace Society, introduced a resolution on compulsory arbitration into the House of Commons which, although rejected, led to a six-hour-debate and attracted respectable support.[73] In the following year the American Peace Society succeeded in getting the Senate Foreign Relations Committee to report a resolution in favor of arbitration to the Senate.[74]

With Richard Cobden, who threw his energies into the cause of peace after his triumph against the corn laws, the crusade moved beyond evangelism into the larger world of politics and foreign policy. Cobden and Cobdenism will be treated further in the final chapter. Suffice it to say here that in the fifties the peace crusade languished. In England, enthusiasm for Garibaldi brought a conflict of loyalties and the Crimean War was a blow to facile optimism; in America the slavery controversy, with its increasing preoccupation with the use of force, took precedence. Yet the crusade had made its mark. An Anglo-American public had been made conscious of the issue and its possibilities; permanent machinery for agitation had been established, and in the cause of arbitration, Judge Jay's thoughtful drafting, Joseph Sturge's organizing genius, Elihu Burritt's evangelistic fervor, and Richard Cobden's deft political lobbying combined to achieve the insertion of an arbitration clause in the Treaty of Paris after the Crimean War.

4. Freedom for Slaves and Women

WHEN Joseph Sturge visited the United States in 1841 in the cause of international peace, he also had a second Quakerly concern which he considered equally important: the abolition of American slavery.[1]

Slavery had always been the outstanding issue of conscience for evangelicals. John Newton, the evangelical preacher who gave spiritual guidance to the Clapham sect, had seen the light as a slave-trader on the Middle Passage and had directed Wilberforce and the others towards their campaign against the trade. The abolition of the slave trade in the British Empire in 1807 was the high achievement of the evangelicals. The successful campaign with its novel methods for swaying public opinion brought evangelicals into the limelight, and, more than any other missionary work, set the pattern for philanthropic radicalism. As has been seen, the techniques employed before 1807, were the model, not only for the subsequent campaign against slavery itself, but for a whole congeries of revivalistic campaigns in Britain and America.

Slavery was also peculiarly relevant to the Atlantic connection. It was a prime economic factor in the Atlantic, and both West Indian islands and Southern mainland shared its effects. Consciences were stirred against the institution at about the same time in England and America. In the last quarter of the eighteenth century the Society of Friends, outside the American South, set its face against slaveholding. Even before the American Revolution, a Philadelphia

Quaker, Anthony Benezet, conducted a campaign against slavery in correspondence with British notables, and wrote tracts which circulated widely in England. His *An Historical Account of Guinea* helped convert the young Clarkson to the cause.[2] The abolition of the trade, which sent the merchants of Liverpool, Lancashire and Newport, Rhode Island, scurrying in search of alternative forms of enterprise, was the almost simultaneous achievement of Britain and the United States. Unlike the British, however, the United States Government failed to take effective steps to put down slave trading and refused to grant to the British the right to search American ships. As a result, the Atlantic slave trade survived, largely as an American enterprise. The initiative against the trade remained with Britain.

The campaign against slavery itself was also directed by British evangelicals and Quakers, and its theatre was the British West Indies. Here resistance was less and the driving force greater, than on the American continent. The power of the West India sugar interest in British politics declined as its plantations became less economic and newer forms of overseas enterprise competed for favors. Colonial slavery in the hands of only sixty thousand whites proved a less difficult problem than the domesticated slavery of the American South with its six million whites; and a sovereign, imperial Parliament could make changes which were not open to the limited Federal Government of the United States. The influence, single-mindedness, and intelligence of British antislavery leaders had no parallel in the United States where the Society of Friends, who were so important to the British cause, shied away from so controversial a topic. In America, gradualism, and the red herring of African colonization remained the order of the day, and when victory came on the West Indian front, the demand of Lancashire for American cotton had so fastened slavery on the American South that the problem of its abolition was intractable.

The British antislavery movement was oriented towards the Atlantic, and drew its strength from those classes in British society with the greatest affinity to the United States. The movement recruited leaders from the evangelical, upper-middle class, notably such men as Zachary Macaulay, his son Thomas Babington, and the Stephen family, one of whom, James, drafted the Emancipation Act and proved a powerful ally in the Colonial Office; but it drew on much more popular support. As the American abolitionist, James G. Birney, was to discover, "the bone and muscle of the anti-slavery cause in this country . . . are the Friends and the Independents. The Baptists as well." [3] And as a Scottish newspaper editor wrote to a West Indian colleague, "All the Dissenters and what is called the evangelical party of the clergymen of the Established Church are enlisted and embarked in the cause against you. Their exertions and influence are very great." [4] This influence was indeed great; for the membership of the Non-conformist and evangelical rank and file was to be found in the middle, and lower-middle classes. As Wilberforce knew by 1825, "It is by the union of people of the middle class of society, amongst whom are comprised the greatest portion of virtue and understanding in every community, that we hope to render our cause successful." [5] Agitation of this element in British life abolished slavery in the West Indies.

During the protracted, sometimes languishing, campaign of a quarter of a century before 1833, antislavery leaders perfected those techniques for mobilizing middle-class opinion for legislative purposes which were to be a permanent innovation in British politics.

The first thing was to establish the facts. Dissenters were

great readers, and not least among the antislavery innovations was a herculean research into the conditions of West
Indian slavery, financed largely by Quaker bankers and merchants. This was embodied in pamphlets which, though often
polemical, marshalled facts and figures like a blue book.
These were distributed to a large reading public which had
hitherto never felt itself to be in the know about great political matters. From 1823 onwards the British Anti-Slavery Society, by means of pamphlets and its own *Anti-Slavery
Monthly Reporter* conducted a paper war against the West
Indian planters of modern dimensions. During 1823 alone
nearly a quarter of a million pamphlets were distributed.[6]
As an American admirer was to put it, with an echo of Mr.
Gradgrind:

We know that it was the exposure of FACTS with regard to the
African Slave Trade which first roused the heart of Clarkson . . .
and that facts, FACTS, have set in motion all that machinery in
England which has at last worked out a peaceful and glorious
deliverance for 800,000 slaves.[7]

But facts alone, it seemed, were not enough to galvanize
the British public to act against slavery. It was not enough
for conventional people to deplore the existence of the institution and to satisfy a charitable conscience by contributing
to the Anti-Slavery Society; it was not enough for Canning to
introduce Parliamentary resolutions for the amelioration and
gradual abolition of slavery. Towards the close of the decade, the more radical antislavery spirits, abandoning gradualism, became convinced that only a demand for immediate
abolition uttered in season and out of season, was likely to
produce results. The demand was justified on moral grounds,
by that doctrine of a "higher law" which Lord Brougham
preached long before it was taken up by American abolition-

ists; [8] and the resulting spirit was more that of an evangelical crusade than a political campaign.

To voice this demand, the Anti-Slavery Society stepped up its publicity. "Practically nothing in the field of modern propaganda was overlooked," wrote the historian of the movement.[9] With money and prodding from the Quakers James Cropper and his son-in-law, Joseph Sturge, a British Agency Committee was established in 1831, under the direction of George Stephen, to drive the campaign. In addition to the pamphlet war, the Committee employed six paid agitators to speak to religious groups up and down the country. These, and especially one, George Thompson, an agitator of great rhetorical gifts and personal magnetism, were responsible for the formation of hundreds of new antislavery societies which organized meetings and speakers, compiled circulation lists, distributed tracts, drafted petitions to Parliament, boycotted slave produce, and raised funds by holding bazaars and fairs. The Committee also copied their West Indian opponents in organizing a placard campaign to reach those who could not read blue books but could spell out a few well chosen sentences.[10] For imagination and thoroughness, the organization could not have been bettered. As Raymond English puts it in his able, unpublished study of Thompson, "A central committee controlling policy, publications and funds, with hundreds of local auxiliary societies to stimulate and discipline the converts, in Britain this was to become the framework of party organization." [11] With the weight of this agitation behind them, and by means of clever debating at Westminster, the antislavery lobby succeeded in 1833 in forcing the Government to introduce a bill which, though not altogether to their liking, abolished slavery in the West Indies.

However, the antislavery zealots by no means rested on

their oars. Slavery must now be abolished throughout the
world, and especially, where it loomed blackest, in the United
States. For had not John Wesley on his deathbed written to
Wilberforce, "Go on, in the Name of God and in the power
of His might, till even American slavery, the vilest that ever
saw the sun, shall vanish away before you"? [12]

West Indian emancipation caught the imagination of kindred spirits in the United States. In 1833 antislavery sentiment was still canalized into the American Colonization
Society's scheme, supported by slaveholders, for exporting
free and freed Negroes to Liberia.[13] Only a handful had followed along the British path from gradual emancipation
(and emigration), to immediate abolition and of these, William Lloyd Garrison, who had recently launched the *Liberator* and the New England Anti-Slavery Society, was a lonely,
if strident, voice. The West India Emancipation Act not only
gave heart to incipient abolitionists, but provided them with
a plan of action. American abolitionists never tired of pro-
claiming their debt to the British movement. "The abolition
movement in America," said the ex-slave, Frederick Douglass, "was largely derived from England," adding later, with
characteristic American reservations, "surely in this sense it
ought to be no disgrace to be an Englishman, even on the
soil of the freest people on the globe." [14] August 1, Emancipation Day, was annually celebrated in antislavery circles
until the Civil War, with warm expressions of amity towards Britain.[15]

The Emancipation Act prompted Arthur Tappan, Joshua
Leavitt and Henry C. Wright in the same year to form the
American Anti-Slavery Society in Philadelphia self-con-
sciously on the British model.[16] Even before the bill was
passed, the importunate Garrison had appeared in London
to solicit support from the British society for the American

cause and to counteract the fund-raising efforts of Elliott Cresson, emissary of the hated American Colonization Society. While in London, where he breakfasted with the antislavery chiefs-of-staff, and walked behind Wilberforce's bier to Westminster Abbey, Garrison decided that what the cause especially needed in America was the services of the ace agitator George Thompson, and he determined to import him.[17] Some of the more conservative British leaders like Clarkson and Sturge were dubious about the propriety of so direct an intervention in the affairs of another country. However, like other antislavery zealots, Garrison and Thompson, who became lifelong friends, were fanatics who recognized no barriers, international or domestic, to moral agitation.

"In moral questions, I say, there are no nations," said Phillips.[18] "Our country is the world, our countrymen are all mankind. We love the land of our nativity only as we love all other lands,"[19] affirmed Garrison; and Thompson said, "Ours is a peaceful remonstrance with America for her sins.... We resort ... but to moral influence."[20] In the delicate question of importing British influence into the United States, all would have seconded Frederick Douglass when he said:

the growing intercourse between England and this country by means of steam-navigation ... gives us an opportunity to bring in the aid ... of those living on the other side of the Atlantic.... We entreat our British friends to continue to send in their remonstrances across the deep against slavery in this land.[21]

Sharing such sentiments, Thompson was not squeamish about using his powerful gifts to stir up in a foreign country an issue which threatened the balance of society and politics at its most delicate point.

English visitors to the United States were curious about slavery, even to the lengths of a morbid fascination with slave auctions. But although a minority, like the Mrs. Maury who was concerned about the servant problem, were in favor of the institution, most were hostile.[22] If the stray remarks of a traveling bookseller could earn him a whipping in Virginia in 1832, and those of an English actor could attract an antislavery mob to the Bowery Theatre in 1834, the advent of an English antislavery agitator in the same year was bound to bring trouble.[23] George Thompson's visit to the United States, in 1834–5, ended with his ignominious exit by rowing boat to a New Brunswick-bound brig.[24] By his rhetorical gifts, and his tactless energy he succeeded, almost single-handed, in provoking the first great wave of Southern bitterness against Northern interference, and in giving the antislavery movement a foreign and alien character. He became, indeed, so notorious as to be the object of a reference in President Jackson's Message to Congress to "emissaries from foreign parts who have dared to interfere in this matter." [25] But in the narrow sense he did much for the cause. He saved the *Liberator* from extinction; his exposure to mob violence in New England provided a new object of hero worship for those with the temperament of martyrs; and during his indefatigable journeys and speeches, he did for the Northeastern States what he had done for Britain. His visit coincided with a phenomenal growth in local antislavery societies, which numbered five hundred by 1835; and it seems likely that his oratory, in over two hundred addresses, was responsible for several hundreds of these auxiliaries which, like their British counterparts, were federated to the national antislavery society, held meetings and fund-raising fairs, distributed tracts, and drafted petitions to state legislatures and Congress.[26] In all this activity, British influence was paramount. When John Quincy Adams embarked on his brilliant, political second childhood as the abolitionist Congressman from Massachusetts responsible for presenting antislavery petitions he was accused of being in league with British abolitionists.[27]

After Thompson's departure, the American Anti-Slavery Society carried its organization a stage further in the direction of the British model. In 1837 it set up an Agency Committee, not of six like the British Committee, but, with Yankee exuberance, of seventy paid antislavery lecturers. The director of "The Seventy" was Theodore Weld, late of the Lane Seminary, who had been converted to abolition by another British evangelical, Captain Charles Stuart. Stuart had returned to the United States in 1834 slightly ahead of Thompson, armed with a presentation to Prudence Crandall from British antislavery ladies and with one thousand dollars for a manual labor school in New Haven. He was an eccentric character. An officer in the East India Company service, he had fought under Wellington, and had retired to Canada, and later to western New York, where he had taught school. He was a strange figure who "wore on all occasions and at all seasons a Scotch plaid frock with a cape reaching nearly to his elbows." At Utica, in 1824, he was converted by Brother Finney to evangelical Christianity, and there he befriended the young Theodore Weld, putting him through the Oneida Institute and concerning himself passionately with his spiritual welfare. In 1829 Stuart went to England on temperance matters, there became converted to antislavery, and, like Thompson, was made a lecturer for the British Agency Committee. His pamphlets, *The West India Question,* and *Thoughts on African Colonization,* proved a powerful influence in the United States in favor of immediate abolition and against gradualism. He was instrumental in converting Weld to the antislavery cause. "I want to have my Theodore's soul engage in the anti-slavery struggle," he wrote to his protégé. "My soul thirsts after you, beloved Theodore. . . . How is your soul?" Stuart remained an important, conservative member of the British Anti-Slavery Society, and for his services the British antislavery leaders arranged his half-pay promotion to Major. Although he lived to despair of Weld's soul, he spent the following thirty years flitting between Canada, the United States, and the British Isles in various good works, including relief during the Irish famine, and toward the end of his life helped finance John Brown's campaign in Kansas.[28]

The violence offered to the abolition cause, in the persons of Thompson, Garrison, Stuart, and others even in the North created a sensation in British antislavery circles. The story was brought home to them by Harriet Martineau in her *Westminster Review* account which she called "The Martyr Age in the United States"; for she had seen the mob assembling in Boston to tar and feather Garrison and Thompson, and had subsequently been forced by conscience, and perhaps a personal yearning for martyrdom, to declare herself an abolitionist, at some expense to her American connections.[29] Meanwhile the Anti-Slavery Society, having in 1838 secured the abolition of the apprenticeship system which replaced slavery in the West Indies, was looking for new fields to conquer. As early as the year of Emancipation, Joseph Sturge had written to William Forster:

Some of my ideas, so far as they have assumed a tangible shape, are these: That a Society should be at once formed for the abolition of slavery throughout the world. . . . The effect of this example throughout the American continent will no doubt be great. . . . Let us therefore form a general crusade against this accursed system throughout the civilized world.[30]

Six years later Sturge and others re-deployed the antislavery forces as the British and Foreign Anti-Slavery Society, with no less an object than world abolition. This meant above all the abolition of American slavery. In practical terms the primary object was to co-operate with the American Anti-Slavery Society in its efforts against the institution in the Southern States. Thenceforward the two national Societies maintained close relations, reinforced by correspondence between Sturge in London and Birmingham and Lewis Tappan in New York, by the exchange of intelligence, pamphlets and newspapers, and virtually annual visits across the Atlantic.[31] As with the sister crusades of peace and temperance, the crown of this benevolent organization was the "World Anti-Slavery Convention." Two of these largely Anglo-American affairs were held in London; the second, in 1843, was a pallid successor to the first, more famous and important Convention, held in 1840.[32]

June, 1840, was a moment of high excitement for the friends of the slave. There gathered in the Freemasons' Hall, Great Queen Street, between five and six hundred delegates, including not only the stalwarts of British evangelicalism but fifty-three delegates from American antislavery societies who had crossed the Atlantic to take part in such a week of debate, resolution-drafting and moral exhortation as the world of Exeter Hall had never before enjoyed. Sturge organized it; but the Americans conceived the idea and the chief object was to mobilize Anglo-American opinion against American slavery.[33] Resolutions were passed in favor of boycotting slave-grown produce and substituting the "free" cotton of India for Lancashire's intake from the American South; but the true theme of the convention was set by the aged Clarkson whose opening speech concentrated on the conscience of the Southern planter.[34] For what the Americans chiefly wanted was the heavy artillery of British moral support.

"I hardly exaggerate," Phillips had written to Thompson

the previous year, "when I say that the sympathy and brotherly appeals of British Christians are the sheet anchor of our cause" and, to underline the authority which Britain still exercised in the intellectual and moral realms, he went on:

England . . . is the fountain-head of our literature; the slightest censure, every argument, every rebuke on the pages of your reviews, strikes on the ear of the remotest dweller in our country. . . . In the name of the slave, I beseech you, let literature speak out, in deep, stern and indignant tones.[35]

This argument was repeated at the Convention by Henry B. Stanton who considered the British reviews the best means of bringing the opinion of the civilized world into the South. It permeated the debates.[36]

This effort to mobilize opinion against slavery concentrated on the Churches. The Americans hoped to shame the South by isolating her from the Christian community, and they were worried about the fraternal relations, cemented by some recent transatlantic visits, between British denominations and their co-religionists in the South.[37] Pressure was therefore brought to bear on the Churches to withhold membership from slaveholders. Resolutions to this effect were transmitted to the leading British and American denominations; [38] and Clarkson in his eightieth year was prompted to write his *Letters to the Clergy of the Various Denominations and to the Slave-holding Planters in the Southern Parts of the United States*.[39] The chief Non-conformist Churches in Britain—the Wesleyan Methodist Conference, the Congregational Union, and the Baptist Union —did their duty that same summer; [40] and during the next few years the Churches held to their antislavery position, which was reinforced in 1846 by the British branch of the Evangelical Alliance.[41] But the subject remained controver-

sial, as was seen in 1844 in the case of the newly formed
Free Church of Scotland which had need, financial and moral,
of close liaison with the American Presbyterian Church in
the South as well as in the North.[42]

Approaching the American denominations was a more
delicate matter. Even the Society of Friends, though committed to antislavery, shrank from radical abolition, and
proved a sorrow to their more militant members, especially
in Britain where their scruples were not understood. English
Friends were shocked to discover that colored people were
segregated in Meeting, and concerned at the lack of response
to hortatory minutes sent to American Meetings. A tactful
epistle to North Carolina Friends ran: "We can sympathise
with you in your difficulties and trials on (the slaves') behalf,
but we hope that you will not be weary in welldoing." [43]
Joseph Sturge's third object in visiting the United States the
year after the Convention was to stir American Friends on
the issue.[44] The Unitarians, also, though finally approving
such a resolution in 1844, considered a memorial from the
British Unitarians as an impertinence.[45] As for the major
denominations, the slavery conflict which led in the case of
the Methodists and Baptists to schisms between Northern
and Southern churches in 1842 and 1845, was exacerbated by
the resolutions of the World Anti-Slavery Convention of
1840.[46]

However, the most striking fact about the Convention was
the changed temper of the Anglo-American connection on
slavery. Henry B. Stanton expressed it when he told the Convention, "To be an abolitionist in England and in America
are very different things; and if I may be permitted to say so,
but a few of your abolitionists have stood the fire on our side
of the Atlantic." [47] Five years earlier British antislavery men
and women had stood the fire. Since then, however, an Amer-

ican generation of radical abolitionists had been exposed to implications of conscience far beyond British experience. After all, Exeter Hall was to survive in the Strand until the twentieth century; but Pennsylvania Hall in Philadelphia had been burnt down within a few days of its dedication by a howling proslavery mob. Harriet Martineau experienced the contrast in tension. "When I returned home," she wrote, "the daily feeling of security and of sympathy in my anti-slavery views gave me a pleasure as intense as if I had returned from a long exile, instead of a tour of recreation." [48] To be an abolitionist in Boston, Philadelphia or Cincinnati meant courting social ostracism, business ruin and physical assault; it called for qualities of personal courage and character which should not be minimized, however foolhardy and short-sighted the single-mindedness which went with it. For Americans, slavery was in the back yard and the color problem in the kitchen and the meeting house. In American eyes, British antislavery was drawing room philanthropy. As one American wrote home to his wife: "These anti-slavery men do not burn with the fire of real enthusiasm like that of our own faithful and sterling friends. Their emancipation is but a political, parliamentary one. It has no heart in it compared with ours." [49] In British eyes, he and his fellow American delegates in London had the glamor, if not of martyrs, of front-line fighters with personal experience of slavery and persecution. For drawing room philanthropists, Garrison was a celebrity, and ex-slaves like Remond and, later, others like Douglass, were objects of devout lionizing. In England's Romantic Age they represented the Savage who had only to be released from his chains to become a free and noble man.[50]

It was little wonder that some of the Americans expressed convictions so radical as to crease the brows and flutter the bosoms of their British brothers and sisters in philanthropy, as well as those of their more conservative fellow country-men. In the apocalyptic vision of this radical minority among the Americans, antislavery was only one aspect of a more universal philosophy of reform which embraced or came to embrace, not merely the respectable trinity of peace, temperance and missionary work, but rights for women, anti-clericalism, perfectionism, nonresistance, and in general a kind of moral anarchism far removed from the theological and disciplinary orthodoxy of Exeter Hall. This universalist spirit had so worked its leaven in the American antislavery movement that before the World Convention the "come-outers," led by Garrison, Nathaniel P. Rogers and others, had persisted in imposing their ideas on the American Anti-Slavery Society. Packing the annual convention at New York in May 1840 with a steamboat load of sympathizers from New England, they had captured the American Anti-Slavery Society for women's rights, and forced the majority of delegates to withdraw to form a new organization, the American and Foreign Anti-Slavery Society, geared directly to the more limited British model.[51] The feminist aspects of this conflict will be considered later. Suffice it here to observe that the Garrisonians contributed to a similar controversy in British antislavery circles.

The great majority of British evangelicals, led by Sturge and the Quakers, wishing to keep strictly to antislavery, held aloof from Garrison's "April's Fool" party, and for the next twenty years remained loyal to the conservative, so-called "New Organization," the American and Foreign Anti-Slavery Society.[52] But a few of the more intellectually lively, including those like Harriet Martineau who were not evangelical and others of a younger generation who were beginning to react against the narrow piety of their fathers, responded to the magnetism of Garrison and his universalist ideas. The

Garrisonians, therefore, continued to enjoy a hearing in Britain, and representatives like John A. Collins spent some time traveling and raising funds there. A portrait of Garrison had an honored place in Harriet Martineau's library at Ambleside.

However, 1840 proved to be the high-watermark of Anglo-American agitation against slavery. For one thing philanthropic agitation, like many things in that hard Victorian world, depended on the trade cycle, and by 1841 the evangelical bankers and merchants whose golden guineas and dollars had financed it were hard-pressed by the stringencies of depression. But apart from this, where could a movement based on moral exhortation go after a world convention? An Atlantic opinion had been organized against slavery, as against drink and war; but it was singularly ineffective in bringing its general abolition. Many of the leaders, and especially the Garrisonians, were by temperament moral agitators who trusted only to the roused conscience of the world and, like Wendell Phillips, refused to soil their hands with politics.[53] Of the more "practical" souls, some, especially the Quakers, were opposed by religious conviction to the use of force, as in the employment of the antislavery squadron of the Royal Navy. The British and American societies collaborated during the forties to lobby Foreign Office and State Department on such issues as the protection of fugitive slaves in Canada and Negro seamen in Southern and West Indian ports, as in the *Amistad* and *Creole* cases.[54] The British antislavery lobby supported the Aberdeen Government in its attempt to maintain Texan independence, in the hope of preserving that State from the full blight of Southern slavery; but such were the limits imposed by nationalism upon Anglo-American opinion that rumors of British intervention only served to overcome Northern resistance to annexation. The concrete results of the 1840 demonstration of sentiment were not impressive.

More practical spirits in each country sensed this, and turned their energies towards linking antislavery to broader political issues: in Britain to the radical attack on the establishment through Chartism or the Anti-Corn Law League, in the United States to an attack on the South by aligning sectional interests, North and West, against it. In both countries the inexorable demands of domestic politics and society pulled the Atlantic movement apart. Henceforward, although the two antislavery societies collaborated, the Garrisonians conducting a bitter guerrilla warfare on the side, the effervescence had subsided, the belief that immediate wonders could be performed by the holding up of hands, had waned.

And yet this Anglo-American movement had perhaps accomplished more than appeared. Whatever the role of abolitionists in America in bringing about the alignment which led to civil war, the antislavery movement in Britain had made popular opinion aware of the evils of American slavery. During the first year after its publication in 1852, *Uncle Tom's Cabin* sold only 150,000 copies in the United States; but in Britain it sold over a million; and the book's exploitation, on stage, waxworks, penny magazines and other mass media, was a phenomenon of the time.[55] This manifestation was general and, to some extent, ephemeral; but antislavery sentiment was to have more lasting effects. Entering the radical system, it so instilled prejudice against slaveholding that the American issue could always provoke a reaction, especially among radical middle, and lower-middle class, chapel-going folk.

The alignment of British opinion towards the American Civil War was more complex than was once supposed. It is difficult to find any positive affinity among the ruling classes for the plantocracy, let alone for slavery itself; the sentiment in favor of Southern independence, deriving from a sense of liberty and self-determination as well as from hostility and fear towards Yankeedom, was by no means confined to the establishment, but included elements among the middle, and even the working, class. At no time was the Government prepared to risk war with the North by mediation which would involve recognition of Southern independence.[56] Yet with all these qualifications, it would still appear that the convictions held about slavery by middle, and working classes, and especially their non-conformist element, were a powerful determinant of opinion. Those convictions only became fully explicit after the Emancipation Proclamation had given earnest that the War was against not only planters but slavery itself; but both political parties had to reckon with them from 1861 onwards. Finally, these convictions were a consistent and deep-seated response on the part of those who had been educated to regard slavery as the enemy of American democracy, and American democracy as the ally of, and example to, reform in Britain. And in so far as Lancashire cotton operatives took the lead in upholding the Union blockade, though this meant the bitter hardships of a cotton famine, it could be said that the crisis revealed the elements of a genuine Atlantic connection, transcending the economic self-interest of the United Kingdom.

The antislavery crusade represents the climax of philanthropic radicalism in the Atlantic world. But no account would be complete which did not include a related phenomenon: the emergence of feminism.

Aristocratic society of the eighteenth century had tolerated an independent role for clever, "strong-minded" women, especially if they had a literary bent like Lady Mary Wortley-

Montagu; enlightened Dissenting families, forced to think out for themselves the proper upbringing of children, educated daughters on a par with sons, just as some Americans of John Adams' generation accepted the equality of their womenfolk in the Revolutionary cause; and in both countries the tradition persisted into the nineteenth century.[57] In England the literary spinster was an accepted, if eccentric, social phenomenon. Whether of aristocratic, or more often Dissenting, background, women like Harriet Martineau, Mary Howitt, Amelia Opie, and Anna Jameson made their own way in the world as journalists or novelists and they had American counterparts, especially in Boston, like Lydia Maria Child, Maria Weston Chapman, and Margaret Fuller, with whom they sometimes maintained relations. Harriet Martineau entrusted to her close friend Maria Chapman the editing of her autobiography; and Lydia Maria Child dedicated *Letters from New York* to Mary Howitt.[58] This incipient feminism had its militant theorist in Mary Wollstonecraft, who was followed a generation later in America by Margaret Fuller, and its propagandist in Frances Wright; and though few literary spinsters took such extreme ground, preferring to promote the cause by the example of their careers, by fostering women's education and safeguarding women's property rights, many held pronounced feminist views.[59]

This tendency of the Enlightenment was inhibited for a generation by the onset of evangelicalism, which sharply reduced women to clinging vines. Yet within the limits of a narrow theology and social convention, women began irrepressibly to exert themselves in humanitarian endeavor. Although Hannah More, member of the Clapham sect, set the evangelical tone for women in America as well as in England, the convention of the lady bountiful allowed her to organize Sunday schools, and distribute tracts, and later

Elizabeth Fry, born a Gurney, to pursue her more ambitious career among the felons of Newgate.[60] And there were to be American equivalents, like Dorothea Dix and Catherine Beecher.[61] But these were exceptionally "strong-minded" women. Most who sought public outlet for their energies did so through the organizations of Exeter Hall. Women played their part in the peace crusade.[62] In temperance, where women best knew the problem of the drunken husband, their influence was even stronger. Women's auxiliaries in Britain, Daughters of Temperance and Martha Washington societies in America, did man's work; and several of the early feminist leaders, including Susan B. Anthony, Abby Kelley, Amelia Bloomer in America, and later Margaret Bright in England, were also active in the cold water crusade.[63] Probably their greatest influence was, however, in the antislavery movement.

From the start women had been the backbone of British antislavery. Without them slavery would hardly have been abolished in the British West Indies in 1833. "The women of England," said Daniel O'Connell at Exeter Hall, "have led the way, and under the banner of the maids and matrons of England proud must that individual be who shall have an opportunity of telling them 'at your command we have done our duty and slavery is at an end.' " [64] Although it was unthinkable that they should be members of antislavery societies, they were encouraged by matinee-idol agitators like George Thompson to form ladies' auxiliaries by the score. The women raised important funds through sales of work, held meetings of women, although addressed and chaired, of course, by men, and, to the surprise of their fathers and husbands, developed talents for committee work and for drafting petitions to Parliament, addresses, and pamphlets. Thomas Fowell Buxton, Joseph Sturge and Joseph Pease acquired efficient, unpaid secretaries in their daughters. Members of

Parliament, Ministers, even the Queen, were embarrassed
by the novel experience of receiving shoals of petitions from
"Her Majesty's Loyal and Affectionate Female Subjects." A
modest, middle-aged Quakeress of Leicester called Elizabeth
Heyrick in 1824 published a tract entitled "Immediate, Not
Gradual Emancipation," which became a major document.[65]
By its vehement argument that progress could be made only
through an insistent demand for immediate emancipation on
moral grounds and irrespective of expediency, this pamphlet
helped change antislavery policy in England and America.
As one American woman put it, "Has not the one idea that
rose silently in Elizabeth Heyrick's mind spread until it has
almost become a world's idea?" [66]

Women were no less forward in America. In 1833 Lydia
Maria Child lost her market as a best-selling author and her
membership of the Boston Athenaeum, by publishing her
influential *Appeal in Favour of that Class of Africans called
Slaves*. Mrs. Chapman, called by James Russell Lowell "the
coiled up mainspring of the movement," wrote *Right and
Wrong in Boston,* a forceful piece of writing which provided
a text for her friend Miss Martineau's *The Martyr Age in
the United States*.[67] They were greatly encouraged by the
example of the British ladies' auxiliaries, whose energies extended to the New World. The ladies of Edinburgh presented Prudence Crandall with a Bible and concordance after
her experiment with unsegregated schooling.[68] Frederick
Douglass's newspaper, *The North Star,* was financed by British ladies' auxiliaries and capably managed in Rochester,
New York, by a British antislavery daughter, Julia Griffiths.[69]
One of Garrison's objects in visiting Britain in 1833 was to
find out "in what manner female influence has been so
widely secured and so powerfully exerted against slavery,"
and the techniques were quickly applied on his return to

America.[70] George Thompson, whose Atlantic fare was paid by the ladies of Glasgow, was instrumental in forming ladies' auxiliaries which made antislavery propagandists of women who had never thought of stepping beyond the parlor. Angelina Grimké, in Philadelphia, wrote the most powerful antislavery tract of the thirties as her "testimonial of conversion" to the cause by Thompson in 1834.[71] One of the complaints against Thompson in America was that he turned "the weaker heads of women." [72] The biographer of Wendell Phillips was not indeed exaggerating when he wrote: "The ladies composed two-thirds of the membership and did three-fourths of the work" of the antislavery movement.[73]

The immediacy of the cause led American women to improve on the British example. Selling homemade pen wipers and pin cushions, pamphleteering and petitioning Congress became tame matters to women exposed to riots and involved with the underground railway. They quickly learned to run their own meetings with women chairmen and speakers. They became skilled at drafting documents; after a suggestion by Lucretia Mott at the first convention of the American Anti-Slavery Society men turned their heads in curiosity to see the woman who knew the meaning of the word "transpose." [74] In 1837 women shocked respectable opinion by speaking to mixed audiences. These first came, naturally enough, from the Society of Friends, where women habitually spoke in Meeting. Although Lucretia Mott and Elizabeth Buffum Chase found themselves in grievous trouble with the Society for their activities, they acquired self-confidence and experience as its travelling ministers.[75] The Grimké sisters also had Quaker experience behind them when they took their stand on the right of women to speak in public. In 1837 Angelina, a Southerner, proved an effective speaker for the Agency of her future husband, Theodore Weld, and found herself addressing audiences of men and women in New England and New York. "My auditors," she wrote, "literally sit sometimes 'with mouths agape and eyes astare' so that I cannot help smiling in the midst of 'rhetorical flourishes,' to witness their perfect amazement at hearing a woman speak in the churches." [76] Her action led to violent protests by the orthodox clergy against women speaking before "promiscuous assemblies," which took on the proportions of a disciplinary campaign.

"If the vine, whose strength and beauty is to lean upon the trellis-work and half-conceal its clusters, thinks to assume the independence and the overshadowing nature of the elm, it will not only cease to bear fruit, but fall in shame and dishonor into the dust." [77] So ran the famous Pastoral Letter to the Churches of Massachusetts in 1837. As Miss Martineau tartly remarked, "It is wonderful how many of these sermons ended with a simile about a vine, a trellis and an elm." [78]

The success of their experiment in public life, together with the masculine hostility it aroused, led the Grimkés and, less dramatically, other women to associate two separate issues: the wrong of slavery and the duty of women to take an equal share with men in its extirpation. The double conflict involved became fused in their minds as one: the right of all human beings to equality before God and men, whether white or colored, male or female. "All through the anti-slavery struggle," wrote Emily Collins, "every word of denunciation of the wrongs of the Southern slave was, I felt, equally applicable to the wrongs of my own sex." [79] And so, Sarah Grimké was led to publish in 1838 her *Letters on the Condition of Women and the Equality of the Sexes,* and Maria Chapman to write her spirited exhortation to the women of New England: "We are told of our powerful *indirect* influence, our claims on man's *gallantry* and *chivalry*. We would not free all the slaves in Christendom by indirection—such indirection. . . . Let our influence be open and direct." [80]

Such heady doctrine created a spirit of insurgency among antislavery women which took them far beyond the modest activities of their English cousins. In the same year as the Pastoral Letter to the Churches, delegates from female antislavery societies came together in New York in a Women's National Anti-Slavery Convention, to be repeated in the following year at the recently opened Pennsylvania Hall in Philadelphia. Here, it will be remembered, opinion on slavery, color, and women's rights was so highly charged that the new American headquarters of benevolent causes was burnt down by a mob during the convention. In 1839, after previously winning the right to membership of the New England Anti-Slavery Society, partisans of women's rights under Garrison's leadership succeeded in so packing the annual convention of the national society that they secured for women membership of this body also.[81] So it came about that, despite the countermanding of such invitations by Joseph Sturge from London, women were appointed by local antislavery societies as delegates to the World Anti-Slavery Convention, and that a number of American women appeared in June 1840 at the Freemasons' Hall in London, demanding to be admitted as delegates.[82]

The spectacle of these half-dozen American women quietly assuming the rights of Exeter Hall, some in Quaker gray, a few, like Lucretia Mott, of middle-age, though most young women in their twenties, caused consternation. The story of how the women's faction presented their case, how a young wife called Ann Phillips kept her husband to the sticking point with the words: "No shilly-shallying, Wendell!", how they were rejected and relegated behind a curtain, has often been told.[83] The clergy of both countries were overwhelmingly against them; and they were informed that English society would not countenance so unseemly a departure from decorum.[84] It appeared that the modest practices of English-women in antislavery matters had been pushed beyond all bounds by the wildly individualistic excesses of these "un-sexed" American women. In short the women's opponents displayed "all the dogmatism becoming to a masculine man." [85] However, the women were not without sympathizers. James G. Birney may have been driven from his boarding house by the indecorous conversation of Elizabeth Cady Stanton; [86] Elizabeth Fry may have walked out of one door when Lucretia Mott entered another, and may have as pointedly prayed for Mrs. Mott's soul; [87] but Daniel O'Connell approved; [88] Harriet Martineau, who had herself been appointed a delegate of the Massachusetts Female Abolition Society, sent well-wishes from her sickbed, and other English feminists including Lady Byron, Anna Jameson, Amelia Opie, and Mary Howitt, together with radicals like Dr. Bowring and William Ashurst, lent support with Garrison and Rogers from the Convention gallery.[89]

The controversy was a nine-day wonder in high-minded London circles. It also stirred profoundly the women who experienced it. The young Elizabeth Cady Stanton, like Ann Phillips, recently married, shared her indignation with Lucretia Mott, and learned from the older woman ideas which were to shape her life. "I had never heard a woman talk what, as a Scotch Presbyterian, I had scarcely dared to think." [90] As the two went about London, walking arm-in-arm down Great Queen Street, or sitting on a bench in the British Museum, they decided to call that woman's rights convention which ultimately took place eight years later at Seneca Falls, New York.[91] And other young American women, notably two Philadelphians, Mary Grew and Sarah Pugh, showed by their subsequent leadership in the American woman suffrage cause that they had not forgotten the London World's Convention.[92]

Less well known is the impact of the demonstration upon the enthusiastic English women who were present. Elizabeth Pease, whose loyalty to American feminists had begun four years before in correspondence with the Grimké sisters, was the only Englishwoman to argue at the first informal debate over the admission of women, and she remained on terms of close friendship and correspondence with the Motts, the Phillipses, the Garrisons and the Stantons. For her, 1840 was another personal step on the journey towards agitation for woman suffrage in Edinburgh.[93] Mrs. Hugo Reid developed the arguments of 1840 in her influential *A Plea for Women*, published three years later. Ann Knight, the Chelmsford Quakeress who had done much to make the American women's stay in England pleasant, wrote the first of an enormous spate of leaflets on women's suffrage in 1846, and drafted the first public manifesto on the subject in Sheffield in 1851.[94] There was Julia Smith, daughter of the Unitarian William Smith of Norwich who had been Wilberforce's lieutenant in the House of Commons, and aunt, on the one hand of Barbara Leigh-Smith who was to be the first secretary of the Woman Suffrage Association, and on the other hand of the Nightingale sisters who followed with indignation the Convention debate. "Aunt Ju" was a member, along with Lady Byron, Anna Jameson, Mrs. Hugo Reid, and Mary Howitt, of that circle of women who were to encourage their younger colleagues to form the first woman suffrage committee in 1855.[95] The daughters of William Ashurst, the radical solicitor who defended Chartists and entertained Mazzini, all became feminists.[96] Matilda, who was "roused to white heat" by the Convention, became the wife of a radical and the

mother of an executive of the London Society for Women's
Suffrage. Caroline married James Stansfeld, M. P., the Liberal statesman and reformer of the prostitution laws. Stansfeld was converted to feminism as an undergraduate at the
London Convention, along with his friend, and law pupil
to Ashurst, William Shaen who, with Mrs. Hugo Reid was
to be co-founder of the Bedford College for Women.[97] This
catalogue takes on heightened significance when it is remembered that these men and women belonged to interconnecting
social circles in London with the same intellectual ambience
which in 1869 produced John Stuart Mill's *The Subjection
of Women.*

These women, English or American, shared a common
moral and intellectual experience. If antislavery bred feminists, the hostility of the clergy to feminism bred freethinkers. To transgress against Church teaching in so fundamental
an issue as Christian womanliness was grave indeed for that
evangelical generation. But far from being intimidated by
the charge that they had unsexed themselves, these women,
accustomed to relying on conscience rather than authority,
began to doubt the Church's teaching. Their confidence in
the pastorate, already undermined by the schism over slavery,
was shattered. Clerical arguments based upon the Bible only
led women to question the authority of the Scriptures.
"Cousin Gerrit would roll up the whites of his eyes if he
knew what I am reading just now," wrote Elizabeth Cady
Stanton to Gerrit Smith's daughter in 1855.[98] One by one
these women left their Churches for Unitarianism and even
less dogmatic creeds, such as that of the Progressive Friends
of Longwood, Pennsylvania or for a personal belief like
Lucretia Mott's "religion of practical life." Some went further and quietly shed their faith. Like Harriet Martineau
they read Comte, became positivists, and, probing the rela-

tion between metaphysical and physical, turned to pseudo-scientific cults, much as a later generation turned to psychiatry. Most of the women and many of the men mentioned in this chapter practiced one or more of the fashionable cults of the time: the phrenology of Spurzheim and Galt, and of George Combe who lectured in the United States and whose Edinburgh home was an important call for visiting Americans; spiritualism; mesmerism, which brought Harriet Martineau out of a prolonged invalid condition; the vegetarianism of Doctor Graham; temperance; a rational dress for women, for the Bloomer costume was as practical as it was a symbol of strong-mindedness; hydropathy, with cold water cures at Buxton, Derbyshire, and wet blanket baths at Saratoga, New York; fresh air, for opening up stuffy Victorian parlors was both a physical and an emotional tonic; new practices in childbearing and rearing, and in birth control. Such eddies of belief were a significant element in the tide of mid-nineteenth century Atlantic opinion.

It was almost ten years before the resolves of June, 1840 produced results, and these appeared first in the United States. That the battle for female equality had still to be won even within the empire of philanthropic endeavor was shown by the rejection of women, amid disorderly scenes, from the World Temperance Convention of 1853 in New York. But in the year of revolutions, 1848, that small group of pioneer feminists at Seneca Falls, led by Elizabeth Cady Stanton and Lucretia Mott, voiced the first demand for woman suffrage, and this was followed in the next few years by a series of woman suffrage conventions and petitions before State legislatures which brought the issue before the public. They also acted as an example to Englishwomen. A report of the woman suffrage convention at Worcester, Massachusetts in 1850 prompted Harriet Taylor to write "The Enfranchisement of Women," which appeared in the *Westminster Review* in October 1852.[99] Three years later English women responded by organising the first committee to promote woman suffrage; but it was another twelve years before the first petition was presented and the National Society for Women's Suffrage founded; and 1867 was the year in which Elizabeth Cady Stanton was already stumping Kansas in an open buggy to demand an amendment to the State constitution.[100]

English women caught another whiff of the prairie and sensed other possibilities for the advancement of women in 1850 when Barbara Leigh-Smith and Bessie Parkes discovered Elizabeth Blackwell who had come to London, with her newly-won doctor's degree from an obscure medical college at Geneva, New York, to pursue her studies at St. Bartholomew's Hospital.[101] Elizabeth Blackwell was the daughter of an English Non-conformist sugar refiner who had moved his business and family of nine from Bristol to the United States in 1832. Bringing with them passionate antislavery views—Wilberforce was a household god—they made their Long Island home a haven for persecuted abolitionists. In 1838 they moved to Ohio and their father died. Thrown on her own resources at twenty-one, Elizabeth supported herself by teaching. In Walnut Hills, Cincinnati, the family was drawn into the circle of the Lane Theological Seminary, and with the Beecher family, W. H. Channing and others, they formed a sort of Transcendentalist cell in the West, taking their cue from *The Harbinger* and *The Dial*.[102] This atmosphere made feminists of most of the Blackwells. Henry married Lucy Stone, the feminist leader, Samuel married Antoinette Brown the woman preacher, and Ellen and Marion became active suffragettes. Elizabeth determined to open up the career possibilities for women by becoming a doctor. Her difficulties in finding a medical school which would accept her and in overcoming the resistance to a woman practicing medicine at each successive stage of her career are well known. She returned to the United States in 1850 and opened a dispensary which became the New York Infirmary and College for Women. For some time she was undecided about whether to pursue her career in America or England, but in the end chose England. Placed on the British Medical Register in 1859, she encouraged English women like Elizabeth Garrett to medical careers, and ended her long life as Professor of Gynecology at the London School of Medicine for Women.[103] The careers of Elizabeth Blackwell and her younger sister Emily, who followed in her footsteps, were thus the embodiment of this Anglo-American connection in its feminist aspects. A daughter of English evangelical Non-conformity, Elizabeth explored the implications of her heritage in the heady air of Ohio; and when she returned to her "fatherland," as she called it, the self-confidence and independence of mind which America had bred in her made her the leader in London in this crusade for the professional advancement of women. Elizabeth Blackwell is the subject of an entry both in the *Dictionary of National Biography* and the *Dictionary of American Biography*. In her, English and American traits are so intermingled that she may only be regarded as an Anglo-American product.

Despite the career of Elizabeth Blackwell, the World Convention of 1840 marked the high point of transatlantic communication in feminism, as in antislavery. Thenceforward, English and American feminists for a generation went the separate ways determined for them by the differing resistances and political character of the two countries. In the United States, leadership in the fully fledged crusade for women's suffrage passed from Boston literary spinsters and Philadelphia Quakeresses to a younger generation whose interests and outlook belonged, not so much to the Atlantic seaboard as to the West. The earliest woman's rights conventions were held in the States of New York and Ohio; even the Worcester Convention represented Vermont and western New England rather than Boston, and most of its leaders had grown up in what was then the West. No doubt the emotional climate of this famous "burnt-over" area, combined with the less restricted and more dynamic society, had much to do with it. Preoccupied with the position of women in a rapidly changing continental society, American feminists neglected, for a generation, their transatlantic communications. In England also, the crusade of women for careers and for the suffrage was shaped by domestic circumstances. Yet, if British feminism developed independently, it drew its greatest strength from those classes which were closest to the United States in sympathy. Its rank and file were middle-class women, provincial, Non-conformist, commercial and professional in background; and prominent among its leaders were the grand daughters of the Old Dissent, including Barbara Leigh-Smith of the Norwich Unitarians and Bessie Parkes, whose mother was American, whose father, Joseph Parkes, was the Birmingham Radical M.P. and whose grandfather was Joseph Priestly.[104]

5. Cross-Currents in Educational Reform

THE desire for education was common ground for most of the people with whom this study has been concerned. For English Dissenters, as for New England Puritans, education was the basis of salvation; for evangelicals, in a more limited sense, the common school was the corollary of the Sunday School in moral and religious elevation; for Benthamites, a utilitarian education, free from religious dogma, was the basis of sound citizenship; for working men, education was the talisman which led to self-advancement and political power; for socialists it was the means of eradicating the acquisitive instinct; for American democrats it was the logical extension of the Declaration of Independence, and for Victorian radicals the moral improvement of the working class through education was the essential prerequisite to that diffusion of political power which was the object of the attack on the establishment.

The position of education in the two countries was very different. One of the advantages of the United States which the British emigrant guides persistently emphasized was the greater possibility of educating one's children. From early times education had been an important social responsibility outside the plantation colonies. Religious communities demanded educated souls; and in Atlantic outposts book learning was a special talisman. In the Middle Colonies, Church and charities supported a variety of schools; but the greatest advances were made in New England, where as early as the seventeenth century the Theocracy had instituted that system of local, compulsory and tax-supported primary and grammar schools which was to be the pride of New England and the model for America. Very largely as the result of this Puritan tradition, the American attitude towards education had become, by the time of the Revolution, fundamentally different from that of the mother country. Education had become a natural right, enshrined in new, and revised, State constitutions and in the famous provisions of the Land Ordinance of 1785. And by the 1820's and thirties, not only could the States of greater New England boast a proliferation of primary and grammar schools, academies and colleges, but Governor Clinton in New York, Henry Barnard in Connecticut and Horace Mann in Massachusetts, were organising those fully fledged common school systems, state-supported, non-sectarian, universal, compulsory, and free, which were to be one of the key institutions of American democracy.

In England, on the other hand, education remained what it had always been since the Middle Ages, the privilege of a governing clerisy. The establishment had its universities and a few great schools; there were the Dissenting academies, grammar schools for the sons of tradesmen, and a variety of charity and dames' schools; but the lower orders, as a whole, and especially the teeming population of the new industrial towns, grew up with perfunctory schooling.[1] Moreover, most of the early philanthropists and reformers, as they organized Sunday and adult schools, schools for paupers and apprentices, and mechanics' institutes, and pressed for state support for church schools, thought of education, not as a right, but as a means for salvation, or for training sober and industrious workers, or for keeping the lower orders within their station in a new industrial age. And the rising middle class, instead of putting their weight behind a demand for state-

maintained secondary schools, as in the United States, devoted their wealth and energies to the foundation of those
new independent boarding schools which, by moulding their
youth to the pattern of Rugby and Shrewsbury, would qual-
ify them for entry into the governing class. A national, state-
supported system of education ultimately took shape; but it
continued to be thought of, not as the provision of a natural
right, but as the gradual extension downwards of an aristocratic privilege. The idea of a governing establishment remained.

These contrasting attitudes towards education in the two
countries, the one populistic, the other paternal, set limits to
the growth of a common Atlantic tradition. Within those
limits, however, there grew up an important two-way exchange of ideas across the Atlantic. If the Americans took the
lead in the provision of public education, British reformers
responded to their formidable problems with new experiments in educational theory and practice which found ready
acceptance in America.

The story begins in the golden glow of the Jeffersonian
Enlightenment. In 1824 Francis Gilmer arrived in London
to recruit professors for Jefferson's new, non-sectarian university at Charlottesville, Virginia, and circulated copies of
the *Rockfish Gap Report,* which embodied the plans for the
University of Virginia, to British acquaintances, including
Lord Brougham, George Birkbeck and Thomas Campbell,
the poet, who had Virginian connections.[2] This American
example encouraged these predominantly Benthamite reformers in their efforts to create a substitute for Oxford and
Cambridge, with their Anglican religious tests, which would
promote unfettered intellectual inquiry. In 1827 there was
founded that "godless institution in Gower Street," University College, London, and later, the University of London

itself. London University in turn became a model for secular universities in the United States, notably New York University, founded in 1832.[3] Thenceforward the connection of American universities was to be far closer with London than with the more socially prominent universities of the establishment, despite the final abolition of religious tests at Oxford and Cambridge in 1871, and the institution of the Rhodes Scholarships in 1902.[4]

However, our concern is not with the universities so much as with mass, popular education. One suspects that in America children may always have been an object of consideration; but in Britain at the beginning of the nineteenth century, their welfare was still of little account. The first insistent popular demand for education came, not so much on behalf of children or apprentices, as from the adult tradesmen, mechanics, factory hands and miners who flocked to Wesleyan study groups and Sunday schools and pursued a painful self-education in the institutions for adult education which proliferated between 1800 and the 1820's.[5] These were variously described but predominantly as mechanics' institutes. Chief among them were the Glasgow Mechanics' Institution of 1823, which had grown out of lectures in popular science to the Andersonian Institution by Birkbeck, Ure, and others, and the London Mechanics' Institution, founded by Birkbeck and the Benthamite circle on the Glasgow model in the same year.[6] The popularity of these prompted Brougham in 1826 to found the Society for the Diffusion of Popular Knowledge to supplement the educational activities of the individual institutes. This Society published a vast literature of sixpenny pamphlets on natural history, mechanics and kindred subjects and a *Penny Magazine* and an *Encyclopaedia* with enormous sales.

These developments had prompt repercussions across the

Atlantic. In one respect the Americans took the initiative. Mechanics' and apprentices' library societies had been founded in several American ports in 1820, and that of New York prompted the foundation of the Liverpool Mechanics' and Apprentices' Library at the other terminus of the North Atlantic run three years later.[7] But in general the British example gave the lead to the United States. Less than a year after the founding of the London mechanics' institute, the Franklin Institute had been founded in Philadelphia, the first formal course of instruction in the mechanical arts given, and fraternal letters exchanged with the London institute.[8] In 1825 there was first published an *American Mechanics' Magazine* on the direct model of the English *Mechanics' Magazine* at the suggestion of which the London Mechanics' Institution had been founded.[9] In 1823 there had appeared in New England, by way of Russia, an English whitesmith called Timothy Claxton. When working in London in 1817 Claxton had founded a Mechanical Institution which was the precursor of the London Mechanics' Institution, and on settling in Boston in 1826 he organized the Boston Mechanics' Institution (with an inaugural speech by Ralph Waldo Emerson) and launched *The Young Mechanic* periodical, in the same year that a Glasgow Scot, William Russell, launched the *American Journal of Education* which featured prominently the activities of the British institutes.[10] In 1829, the Boston, and in 1836, the American, Society for the Diffusion of Useful Knowledge were founded on the model of Brougham's London society of the same name.[11] This British experience, according to the historian of the movement, provided the background for Josiah Holbrook in his promotion of the American Lyceum.[12]

The mechanics' institutes in England, like the Lyceums in America, had an enormous initial success. As late as 1850 the institutes in Britain were seven hundred in number with 120,000 members.[13] But their original object proved too ambitious. Only a tiny minority were equipped to profit from expert instruction in the mechanical sciences; membership fell rapidly away, and the emphasis shifted to less exacting discussion, lectures on general topics, the provision of newspapers and periodicals and socials. This was almost from the beginning the characteristic program of the American Lyceums, which, by the 1840's, were very largely devoted to providing forums for the popular lecturers of the day; and it was perhaps in recognition of this revised American pattern that there was formed in 1838 in Manchester, and copied elsewhere, a Lyceum, designed to attract "a lower grade of society than that from which the members of the Mechanics' Institutions were generally drawn." [14] Thus in Manchester the movement passed through three phases: the Manchester Athenaeum, of which the young Richard Cobden was a founder-member, and which became a club for manufacturers; the Mechanics' Institute, which was captured by "respectable" shopkeepers and a few self-educated artisans, and the Lyceum, which, it was hoped, would yet provide improvement for the masses.

This hope never materialized in Britain. Workingmen had come to distrust the institutes, not just because they were intellectually over workingmen's heads, but because they were considered agents of the masters. When Brougham organized his "Steam Intellect Society," as Peacock nicknamed it, his object was not merely to impart "useful knowledge" to the mechanic, nor even to tap for society the native inventiveness which intellectuals were just discovering the mechanic to possess, but to indoctrinate him with a proper view of his social duties. Brougham's original article in the *Edinburgh Review* advocated the founding of the Society, on the ground that a diffusion of knowledge would prevent class conflict; and running throughout the Society's publications is an insistence on the rights of capital in the economy.[15] As a result, in Chartist days, English workingmen became alienated and, withdrawing from the mechanics' institutes, organized their own mutual improvement societies such as the National Hall, Holborn, established by William Lovett within his Working Men's Association in 1841.[16] Such societies had a Chartist bias, and set workingmen's education in England on a political course which was to lead to the Workers' Educational Association of the years before the first World War. The point is worth emphasizing since it brings out a contrast between English and American conditions. In America, it is true, the Jacksonian workingmen, like the Chartists, placed education in the forefront of their aims. But the Workies did not consider they belonged to a separate class and felt no militant desire to acquire their own education as an essential political weapon for wresting rights from a ruling class. This lack of motive, combined with the imminence of state education, prevented adult "improvement" taking a political course in the United States.[17]

Bound up with mechanics' mutual improvement was the provision of cheap newspapers and periodicals; and here the American example was paramount. Prominent among the demands of British radicals from the time of Cobbett's *Register* onwards was the removal of the stamp tax on newspapers which was preserved by the Tories as a means of keeping political intelligence beyond the reach of workingmen's pockets. A crusade for the removal of the "taxes on knowledge" became an integral part of the liberal attack on the establishment, and it gained sustenance from the American example of a free press. It was an American, Dr. James R. Black of Kentucky, whose pamphlet helped to launch the Society for

Promoting a Cheap and Honest Press in 1836; [18] and during the successful climax of the agitation in the fifties, the luxuriant foliage of the *New York Tribune,* displayed by Horace Greeley in London, excited wonder and envy even greater than did the *New York Times* Sunday edition to the newsprint-starved British during the recent war.[19] For mid-Victorian radicals, not least among republican institutions was the cheap newspaper.

More important than adult education was the interaction between Britain and America in common schooling. It will be remembered that universal education was a prominent demand of workingmen's parties on both sides of the Atlantic during the 1820's and 1830's, in America as a natural right along with universal suffrage and in England as an essential point in the People's Charter. In particular Robert Owen's experiments among the factory population of New Lanark and the colonists of New Harmony played an important part in shaping the thinking of both Chartists and American workingmen's parties. Robert Dale Owen and Frances Wright inserted their elaborate educational creed of "a National System of Equal, Republican, Protective, Practical Education, the sole Regenerator of a Profligate Age . . . ," into New York politics in 1828; and the Owenite creed remained an important ingredient in English working-class politics. In the long run it also had a profound influence on educational theory in both countries. Owen's original ideas, example, and flair for publicity, were in part responsible for the domestication both in Britain and America of the educational theories of Pestalozzi and Von Fellenberg. More immediately, the New Lanark experiments bore fruit in the education of infants. The founding in 1824 of the London Infant School Society is the first landmark in a successful and characteristically English contribution to educational progress. Even before this, in 1816, the New Lanark idea had reached Boston, where the City Council established infant schools, and in the next decade the example was followed in New York and Philadelphia.[20] In general, however, Owenite education was too utopian, too platonic, and too radical in educational theory to be more than an exotic offshoot of the movement for popular education. More important were humbler and more pragmatic efforts.

One of the chief problems facing philanthropists, especially in relation to the new, teeming industrial population of Britain, was that of finding a method of mass instruction, within both the financial means of private philanthropy and the limited supply of teachers. The earliest attempt to grapple with this intractable problem was the monitorial system whereby the older children taught to the younger the three R's which they had just themselves learned. This proved a short cut and inadequate solution to an overwhelming problem; but it was cheap, limited, could be promoted by private philanthropy, and was therefore comparatively uncontroversial. The two rival systems of Andrew Bell and Joseph Lancaster enjoyed some vogue in England in the early years of the century. The chief difference between the two systems lay in the emphasis on religious instruction. Bell's "National Society for Promoting the Education of the Poor," was Anglican in emphasis and patronage, whereas Lancaster's "British and Foreign School Society," was undenominational. Perhaps because of its Anglican character, the Bell System never caught on in the United States; but the Lancasterian System immediately became popular, and was incorporated into the schools of the New York Free School Society, the charity schools of Philadelphia and elsewhere. In 1818, Lancaster, the Quaker, discouraged by losing the patronage of the rich and powerful to Bell, the Anglican, decided to try his personal luck in the more experimental climate of the United States. He was received with enthusiasm and his system hailed as the solution to the problem of popular education. The Governors of New York and Connecticut recommended the system to their legislatures. De Witt Clinton called him "the benefactor of the human race," believed that his system was "a blessing from heaven to redeem the poor and distressed of this world from the power and dominion of ignorance," and significantly asserted, that "the system operates with the same efficiency in education as labour-saving machinery does in the useful arts." [21] Lancaster, through his treatise published in 1821, and his Lancasterian Institute at Baltimore, exerted considerable influence on schooling in the 1820's. In New York his chief disciple was the Quaker chemist and educator, Joseph Griscom, who in 1818–19 had studied educational practice in Europe, including Robert Owen's New Lanark.[22] But although monitorial schools were established in the principal cities of North America from Washington to Quebec, the system quickly revealed its weaknesses, and was so successively modified as to lose all its distinctive features. Lancaster himself, who was run over in New York in 1838, died in poverty.[23]

The monitorial system was no solution to the problem of popular education either in America or Britain. When Horace Mann studied educational practice in Europe he concluded that although it worked "under such an energetic and talented teacher as Mr. Crossley of the Borough Road School in London," the term "monitorial" had been given to such schools "by way of admonishing the world to avoid their adoption." [24] The problem was more deep-seated and had to be tackled in a less piecemeal manner. It was in part educational, involving a shift from mechanical instruction, as in the monitorial system, to the more imaginative concept of training preached by Pestalozzi; but it was also, in part, a problem of organization, and more specifically of the role of the State.

When Horace Mann became the first Secretary of Education in the State of Massachusetts in 1837, he faced a problem not altogether unlike that which faced Dr. James Phillips Kay on his appointment as Secretary of the Committee of the Privy Council on Education in England two years later. Massachusetts was turning away from her state-supported school tradition. With a growth in wealth and population, new private schools and academies had grown at the expense of the old district arrangements which had become hidebound. If the old New England tradition of public education were to be resuscitated, the district system must be reorganized. A public school system, universal, compulsory, and free, could develop only under forceful control by the State Government.[25] In their great campaigns to this end, as well as to overcome ecclesiastical hostility to secular education, Mann in Massachusetts and Henry Barnard in Connecticut and Rhode Island fought battles which had in the end also to be fought in England. And in this the Americans took the lead.

The crux of the question was state control. When Mann visited Europe in 1843 he ranked the "voluntarist" school system of England the lowest of that of any country he visited.[26] Mann's famous *Seventh Report,* like the previous reports of the Ohioan, Calvin Stowe, and the Frenchman, Victor Cousin, was concerned not with English, but with Prussian education.[27] The English themselves were equally concerned with Prussia and Cousin's work, translated by Sarah Austin, wife of the Benthamite jurist, was influential in reformist circles in Britain as well as in America. But it was the Americans who succeeded in domesticating Prussian methods. Horace Mann's "Massachusetts System" became a model for

British reformers in their drive for a system of public education.

The public, state-determined character of American education, with its school boards and state superintendents, bears testimony to the continuing force of New England Puritanism, without which the populistic drive for education might well have taken the road of private enterprise, like so much else in American life. As it was, the Massachusetts System was an exceptionally appropriate model for England.

Resistances to its adoption were, however, much greater. Not only were some High Tories hostile to the extension of an aristocratic privilege, but those interests which were in favour were at odds about the method of bringing it about. The great stumbling block was religious instruction. In America, the accepted principle of the separation of Church and State weakened the resistance of the Churches to a thoroughly secular system of state education. In England, on the other hand, the supporters of state education among the evangelicals of the Church of England saw it as an extension of the schools of the Established Church, whereas the Dissenters wished to preserve their own tradition and preferred that there should be no public education at all rather than an Anglican state system. The Congregationalist leader, Edward Baines, went so far in his suspicion of the Establishment and his preference for "voluntarism" as to be hostile to all government direction; as he wrote, "The tendency of all things committed to Government is to become stagnant, frozen, bound in chains which it requires a Hercules to break. Is not this the very genius of Downing Street and Somerset House?" [28] As a result of this conflict, the introduction of state education in England was delayed for a generation. When it came, the Education Act of 1870, introduced by W. E. Forster, represented a compromise whereby the Bible should be taught in schools on a non-denominational basis.[29] Within limits, the 1870 Education Act, with its elected school boards, its finance from the local rates and its compulsory powers, bears a great resemblance to the Massachusetts System which, during the previous twenty years, had become a model for educational crusaders.

English visitors to the United States, of whom over three hundred published accounts of their travels between 1824 and 1870, "bore unanimous witness to its educational achievements"; [30] and the Massachusetts System became well known to English radical circles through the press. However, it owes much to the advocacy of particular Englishmen with transatlantic connections. Mention has been made of George Combe, the Scottish phrenologist whose science became so popular among this Anglo-American generation. The interest of George Combe and his brother Andrew in phrenology was linked with an interest in a rational, scientific education. Another brother, Abram, fired by a visit to New Lanark, attempted an Owenite experiment at Orbiston, in Scotland, and George, in 1833 published some lectures, delivered to evening classes, in which he argued against a classical, and in favor of a practical, education.[31] Thenceforward George Combe was in correspondence with educational reformers. When he visited the United States between 1837 and 1839, he became a friend and admirer of Horace Mann, at that time beginning his career as Secretary of Education in Massachusetts. Combe lectured for Mann on education throughout the Commonwealth. "I shall rejoice to sow seeds which Mr. Mann may ripen into a lovely and abundant harvest of morality and intelligence," he wrote.[32] And his enthusiasm for Mann's work knew no bounds. "I could fill many sheets," he wrote to his brother, "with an exposition of the advantage of a Commonwealth when the people are moral and enlightened." [33] Combe corresponded constantly with Mann for the rest of his life. On his return to Britain, although at first he despaired of reforming his countrymen—for, as he wrote, "scientific, clerical and aristocratical prejudices in Britain are more than I feel disposed to encounter"—he determined to make the British public aware of the importance of Mann's efforts in education.[34] His personal advocacy and his articles in the *Edinburgh Review* and elsewhere did much to acquaint the British public with the Massachusetts experiment; and his plan for national education in Britain, published in 1848, which incorporated all the essential features to be found in the Acts of 1870 and 1872, was based on the Massachusetts System.[35]

Combe's exposition of Horace Mann's innovations in the *Edinburgh Review,* for July 1841, was the model for a program of universal education drawn up six years later by Samuel Lucas for a Manchester Committee which became the Lancashire Public School Association.[36] That Lancashire should have taken this lead was not accidental. The Manchester Committee, which included Jacob Bright, brother of John Bright, and Samuel Lucas, who married Margaret Bright, a sister, held its first meeting at the Lloyd Street Chapel which had provided six out of the seven original members of the Anti-Corn Law League.[37] In 1847, the year after the triumphant abolition of the corn laws, Manchester radicals were looking for new fields to conquer, and what could be more logical than the achievement of public education for those industrial classes who were to play so responsible a role in a radical England?

Another person with whom George Combe carried on an indefatigable correspondence was Richard Cobden; and one of Combe's earnest endeavors was to persuade Cobden to seek new laurels in the cause of universal education. "You, my respected friend," he wrote, "in Parliament stand in the position which Horace Mann does in America. You have a *right* to lay bare the nakedness of the existing schools and to urge Parliament and the nation to introduce a better system." [38]

Cobden did not need much persuasion about the importance of either public education or the American example. When in 1835 as a young man he had visited the United States he had recorded in his diary a resolution formed after inspecting an American school:

Oh the happy sight, pregnant with hopes of the exaltation of the character of future generations! I hereby dedicate myself to the task of promoting the cause of infant schools in England where they may become an instrument for ameliorating the fate of the children working in the factories whose case I fear is beyond the reach of all other remedies.[39]

On his return to England he had tried to impress his fellow-countrymen with the fact that "The Americans are the best people . . . because in our opinion the people that are the best educated must, morally and religiously speaking, be the best." [40] There are grounds for thinking that the young Cobden's original aim in politics had been to unite all radical interests in an educational program, based upon American example. In 1836 he had held a meeting in his countinghouse in Manchester, to which ministers of every denomination were invited, to discuss "a system which it was proposed to try to agitate": [41] and two years later he wrote to Tait, the Edinburgh book seller: "Do not let your zeal for the cause of democracy deceive you as to the fact of the *opaque ignorance* in which the great bulk of the people of England are wrapt . . . I hope you will join us in a cry for schoolmasters as a first step to Radicalism." [42]

This original design appears to have been sidetracked by sectarian animosities and the greater power of free trade. However, after his great victory, Cobden once again turned his attention to education. "The settlement of the Free Trade controversy," he wrote to Combe in July 1846, "leaves the path free for other reforms, and Education must come next." [43] And two years later he wrote to the same correspondent: "In my opinion every extension of popular rights will bring us nearer to a plan of National education, because it will give the poor a stronger motive to educate their children." [44] Cobden became a vice-president of the Lancashire Public School Association, and spoke powerfully on its behalf, in and out of Parliament. The American example was never far from his thoughts. In January 1851 he said in Manchester: "Where is our boasted superiority, when the American minister can come to the Town Hall here and taunt us with the ignorance of our people and when nobody dares rise up and say, we have done as much for education as they have in America." [45] And again:

We are the only people that have had voluntaryism and we are behind all the world. But in the United States they don't trust voluntaryism. They make use of their parochial and their municipal organization to secure a system of schools free to all, paid for by all. . . . All classes are educated at the common public school.[46]

And as he asked the House of Commons:

Where is the difficulty of our doing what has been done in Massachusetts? I will not be driven from that ground. Give me the Massachusetts plan. I declare my belief that the mass of the people in Massachusetts are as superior in intelligence to the population of Kent as the latter are to the people of Naples. I say this advisedly. I ask, then, why we cannot have this system in England? [47]

No one knew the difficulty better than Cobden. It was not possible to move a step beyond the support of the Dissenters, for "the main strength of any such movement must be in the Liberal ranks of the Middle Class, and they are almost exclusively filled by Dissenters." [48] Yet, despite the fact that "Mr. Baines and his Dissenting friends," were "as hot as ever" on the subject, by November 1850, Cobden had "made up my mind to go for the Massachusetts system as nearly as we can get it." [49] In this Cobden was the spokesman, not merely for the Lancashire Association, but for the National Public School Association which, in 1850, took its place. It took twenty years for the N.P.S.A.'s efforts to bear fruit in the Education Act of 1870. Yet the essential features of the national system were worked out by 1850 in Manchester, which remained the headquarters of the Association. For those were the days when it was truly said that "opinion in Parliament was far behind Manchester." [50] The work of the N.P.S.A. was well done; and it was influenced by a powerful American example.[51]

6. The Nature and Limits of the Atlantic Connection

THIS study has traced different kinds of communication between Britain and the United States in the early nineteenth century, in trade, investment, and migration, and in political and philanthropic radicalism. The time has now come to pull these various lines together to see if they make a single communications system sufficiently defined to justify using the term "Atlantic Connection"; and, if so, to understand the character of that connection and its limits.

The reader who has had the patience to pursue these highways and byways of Anglo-American relations may have become conscious of intersecting trails, may on occasion have recognized places and people met on earlier expeditions. Or, to put it another way, may have come to recognize the *dramatis personae* of a somewhat untidy, picaresque story, not unlike an eighteenth century novel. It is the relationships among these characters, and the moral problems posed by them, which it is the object of this final chapter to explore.

Not all the characters have borne much relation to each other. Many have been mere walk-on parts; and in many of these relationships, communication has been partial, at best. By no means all merchants and bankers were free traders or philanthropists, nor all emigrants and travelers idealists. The most radical of manufacturers abhorred unions and socialism, just as Chartists and land reformers hated capitalism; and Cobden, the liberal, and O'Connor the Chartist, were at one in opposing emigration for British workingmen. Quakers were uncomfortable partners to "worldly" men in the most unworldly of causes, and William Allen broke with Robert Owen over the music, dancing and military training at the New Lanark schools. Evangelicals, to a man, shunned free thought as the work of the devil; even as liberal-minded an abolitionist as E. S. Abdy believed that Nashoba "has disgusted every man who has any regard for the decencies and duties of life"; [1] and the reciprocal scorn of freethinkers for pious enemies of enlightenment is well displayed by Gilbert Vale's hostile account of an interview with J. J. Gurney.[2] Antislavery enthusiasts from Wilberforce onwards were often impervious to the condition of workingmen. Workingmen were often bitterly hostile to abolitionists. In America the Chartist emigrant, John Campbell, even published a racist pamphlet, entitled *Negro Mania;* and George Henry Evans wrote an open letter to Gerrit Smith accusing him of being a virtual slaveowner since he was the largest landlord in the State of New York. In Britain, workingmen listened to tales of returning travelers which contrasted unfavorably their own condition with that of the slaves, and were suspicious of abolitionists like Harriet Beecher Stowe who hobnobbed with aristocratic landowners and ascribed the poverty of workingmen to drink; [3] and some of the agrarian radicals carried their distrust of industrial capitalism so far that, during the American Civil War, they sympathized with the agricultural, though slaveholding, South.[4] Only a tiny minority of evangelicals sympathized with the feminists and few of the women themselves could swallow all the doctrines of Fanny Wright. Not all abolitionists were pacifists, as the controversy over the use of naval cruisers showed. Not all abolitionists were free traders, nor all free traders abolitionists, and those that tried to be both suffered from a conflict of loyalties, like Sturge and O'Connell who were opposed to the reduction of duties on slave-grown sugar, and Cobden, whose free trade sympathies for the Cotton South for a time neutralized his Northern loyalties at the outset of the Civil War. And yet, even more striking than these differences is the extent to which these groups of opinion shared common ground; and it was a ground common and important to Anglo-American relations.

American delegates to the World Anti-Slavery Convention of 1840 who crossed the Atlantic on the *Great Western* had the idea of pressing for a reduction in the price of the passage on the ground that they were all "cold water drinkers." [5] Preceding chapters have shown the intimate connections, not only between temperance and abolition, but between these and the missionary, peace, and feminist movements on both sides of the Atlantic. At Exeter Hall William Allen, Joseph Sturge, J. J. Gurney, George Thompson and others formed a holding company with interlocking directorates in many fields of moral reform. These men co-operated in gentleman's agreements with their opposite numbers in the United States: with Arthur and Lewis Tappan, Gerrit Smith, William Jay and William Lloyd Garrison; and these humanitarian trusts also had their connections with the wider world of political reform.

In the United States, those connections were less extensive, and more tenuous, than those in Britain. Political radicalism, in the British sense, cannot be easily isolated in America, because the fundamental rights which British radicals were seeking had already been won at the Revolution. There was no easily defined establishment against which to rally all the forces of reform. Furthermore, whereas under the British constitution, power was concentrated in a sovereign Parliament and subject to greater risks and fears, under the Federal constitution, powers were limited and divided; and the sectional character of politics determined that issues should be largely local and disparate. Political radicalism, in the British sense, manifested itself only in a few exotic and isolated Utopias, and in the workingmen's parties of the eastern cities. As regards the Utopias, Nashoba had an antislavery object; both Birkbeck and Owenite settlements were antislavery in sentiment, and the New Harmonists experimented in education and equality between the sexes. But their atheistic temper had nothing in common with that, say, of evangelical Oberlin. Eastern workingmen responded to neither temperance nor pacifism; their response to abolition was often hostile; and, as for the evangelical spirit, their reaction to the working conditions imposed at Tappan Brothers, which included compulsory Sunday and mid-week Church and the policing of private morals, must have been unprintable. The only genuine attempt to align a philanthropic cause with insurgent politics was that of certain abolitionists to link antislavery with free trade in a grand design to shift the basis of the American export trade from cotton to wheat. This is reserved for later discussion.

In Britain the connections between political and philanthropic radicalism were more intimate. Evangelicals and utilitarians were united in prison reform. The crusade for universal education attracted utilitarians, evangelicals, Chartists, Dissenters, and Cobdenite radicals alike. Temperance evoked a strong response among those thrifty artisans and shopkeepers who were attempting to better themselves by attending mechanics' institutes, reading *Chambers' Journal*, joining co-operatives and the like; and it appealed especially to the chapel-going, manufacturing, middle and lower-middle class. James Cluer was both a Chartist and a temperance lecturer, Joseph Livesey both temperance lecturer and an influential member of the Anti-Corn Law League. As

Richard Cobden wrote to Livesey in 1849, "The temperance cause really lies at the root of all social and political progression in this country," [6] and advising Henry Ashworth against the holding of dinners for the Liberal Party he wrote, "I have more faith in teetotalism than in bumper glasses so far as the interests of the democracy are concerned"; for "our strength lies with the shopocracy . . . the teetotalers will be found the best workers in the ranks of the Liberals whilst the drinkers will be the only hope of the Tories." [7] Pacifism also appealed to all who were opposed to the establishment: to Chartists no less than to a middle class who resented being taxed for the upkeep of aristocratic armed forces and a warlike foreign policy which threatened to interfere with trade. It is not surprising, therefore, that Cobden made pacifism, like temperance, a cardinal point in the program of mid-Victorian radicalism:

It has struck me [he wrote to Henry Ashworth] that it would be well to engraft our Free Trade agitation upon the Peace Movement. They are one and the same cause . . . Free Trade, by perfecting the intercourse and securing the dependence of countries one upon another, must inevitably snatch the power from the *governments* to plunge their people into wars. . . . I should like to see the London [Society of] Friends interested in the question of the Corn Law and Free Trade. They have a good deal of influence over the City moneyed interest, which has the ear of the Government.[8]

And later, in a letter to George Combe: "If we can keep the world free from actual war, and I trust railroads, steamboats, cheap postage and our own example in Free Trade will do that, a great impulse will from this time be given to social reforms." [9] And to popular education, temperance and pacifism may be added feminism. For even the incipient feminism

of the antislavery movement found corroboration among the
women who attended anti-corn law meetings on equal terms
with their husbands in the industrial North.

However, the philanthropic reform with the broadest connections was antislavery. It will be remembered that the
World Anti-Slavery Conventions marked the high point of
moral agitation against the institution. Thereafter in England, as in America, abolitionist leaders sought to implement
moral agitation by alliance with other reforms in politics.
Joseph Sturge and George Thompson both flirted with Chartism. Sturge had already lent his influence to the Chartists at
Birmingham in 1838. His Quaker conscience had been
aroused by interrupters at an antislavery meeting demanding
"that slavery at home be first abolished," and after the Bull
Ring riot he wrote: "I am sorry to say that amongst some of
the the middle and higher class with us there is a feeling
almost as bitter towards the working classes as there was towards the slave-owners." [10] His visit to the United States in
1841 convinced him that only a greater measure of democracy
would shift the balance of politics in Britain, and on his return he pursued his Chartist connections further by organizing the Complete Suffrage Association in 1842. This Association, which had its origins at a meeting of the Anti-Corn
Law League in Manchester, was a high-minded attempt to
unite middle and working class radicals. George Thompson,
who had associated with London workmen's groups in the
1820's, also took part in the Complete Suffrage Association;
and in 1846 he pursuaded the "moral force" Chartists, Henry
Vincent and William Lovett, to join him in founding a National Anti-Slavery League which would link the plight of
the slave with that of the workingman. Among its founder
members, characteristically, were the American "April's Fool"
or lunatic fringe abolitionists, William Lloyd Garrison,

Nathaniel P. Rogers, Frederick Douglass and Henry C. Wright, who were then in London.[11] "There is an overwhelming mass of evidence," wrote F. J. Klingberg, "that the English workingmen, becoming conscious of the value of American propaganda and counter-propaganda, were resolved to bring them to bear upon their own desperate political and economic struggles."[12] The long-term results of this identification were to show in the events of the Lancashire cotton-famine.

However, the attempt to unite middle and working class politics proved abortive. The antislavery movement found more powerful allies among middle-class radicals, and indeed became for a time largely absorbed into another reform crusade which the middle class regarded as of overriding importance, namely, free trade.

The dismantling of the mercantilist apparatus and the encouragement of free trade with other countries were patently in the interests of an England whose industries had so marked an advantage over those of the rest of the world. Moreover the classic writers on political economy, from Adam Smith to Mill, who emphasized the "unseen hand" working for social good through a free market, implied an entire social and moral philosophy which was attractive to commercial England. The Manchester School preached a body of doctrines which supported the aspirations of the rising middle classes with moral force. The corn laws especially, which protected the landed interest in their rents, became for both sides the great symbol of aristocratic privilege. For the radicals, their abolition was the one great overriding reform which must come about if the grip of the establishment on Britain were to be loosened and a new, more just society come into being. Cheap bread would raise the standard of living of the work-

ing classes; free trade in corn would lessen the costs of manufacture and bring increased profits by swelling the volume
of international trade. Free Trade became the great rallying
cry of the radicals in their attack on the establishment. As
Richard Cobden wrote to his brother in 1838:

I think that the scattered elements may yet be rallied round the
question of the corn laws. It appears to me that a moral and even
a religious spirit may be infused into that topic, and if agitated
in the same manner that the question of slavery has been it will
be irresistable.[13]

The anti-corn law campaign developed in an Anglo-
American context. From the rise of the Cotton Kingdom,
cotton manufacturers were concerned about the absolute dependence of Britain's great staple industry upon its single
source of supply in the American South, whose publicists
expected Britain "to be a very quiet friend of ours for the
next three or four centuries." [14] Liverpool merchants, such
as John Gladstone, and the Manchester Chamber of Commerce, were advocating the development of alternative sources
of supply as early as the 1820's. This concern was connected
with criticism of the East India Company's monopoly which
was held to interfere with the proper development of India
as a market and source of supply for raw materials. If raw
cotton could be grown in India, Britain would become independent of the American South, and the price of raw cotton
on the Liverpool Exchange would cease to be so highly speculative, related as it was to the one American crop. Connected
with this, also, was a growing awareness in industrial Britain
of the unsatisfactory nature of the Southern economy as a
market for British manufactures. As was seen in Chapter
1, Lancashire was losing the market for coarse, slave clothing, to the tariff-protected industry of New England. In addi-

tion, British business men were growingly aware that an economy of slaves, who had few wants, had grave limitations as a market for consumers' goods. As a Lancashire spokesman had recognized as early as 1821, "Slaves have no wants, but of rest—no desires, but to avoid the lash; and it is only the wants and desires of the comparatively few proprietors that cause a demand for the productions of other countries." [15] Their anticipations turned instead to the growing, free population of the North, and of the new, agricultural Northwest. But if Indian cotton was to be substituted for American, how were the Americans going to pay for the growing volume of manufactures which the British hoped to sell to the North and West? The answer was by exporting wheat instead of cotton to Britain. To revamp the Atlantic economy on these lines needed a greater measure of free trade between the two countries: lower American tariffs to allow British manufactures to compete on even terms with American manufactures, and above all, the abolition of the British corn laws which appeared to prevent the free flow into Britain of the rich yields of the newly settled prairies of the Northwest.[16] Miss Martineau had written in 1837:

The prospects of agriculture in the States northwest of the Ohio are brilliant. The stranger who looks upon the fertile prairies of Illinois and Indiana and the rich alluvions of Ohio, feels the iniquity of the English corn laws, as strongly as in the alleys of Sheffield and Manchester. The inhuman perverseness of taxing food is there evident in all its enormity.[17]

These possibilities were not lost upon the men who met at Manchester in December, 1838, to found the Anti-Corn Law League. They included J. B. Smith, President of the Manchester Chamber of Commerce, which concluded, in its annual report for the following year:

A vast population has grown up in the interior states of the Union, whose surplus production consists of corn and other articles of food. Their voice will go far to determine the cnaracter of the future commercial intercourse between America and this country. If wisdom direct our proceedings, we shall adopt such a policy in regard to import duties upon the natural productions of the United States as will secure to us an increasing commerce with the people of that important country.[18]

And after the cause had triumphed, Cobden's lieutenant, Archibald Prentice, on a visit to New York harbor, could ruminate thus on its Anglo-American implications:

. . . bright visions arise in the imagination of the utilitarian. He sees the farmer on the Hudson, the Mohawk, the Ohio, the Illinois, the Miami and the lakes of Michigan, Erie and Ontario, cheerfully labouring in his own fields for the sustentation of the Manchester spinner and weaver; he sees the potter of Hanley, the cutler of Sheffield, the cloth manufacturer of Yorkshire and the sewer and tambourer of Glasgow, in not hopeless or unrewarded toil, preparing additional comforts and enjoyments for the inhabitants of the American woods and prairies. He conjures up a great co-operative community all working for the mutual benefit; and sees in the universal competition the universal good. He sees the individual and the general advantage combined, and the world as only one vast brotherhood.[19]

It will be seen that the crusade against the corn laws had a special appeal for antislavery men. For it promised to hobble and perhaps strangle slavery by re-directing the energies of the Atlantic economy away from the American South and towards a more natural intercourse between the progressive elements in British and American life; between, on the one hand, a middle-class, business, non-conformist, evangelical Britain, and on the other, its cousinhood in the northern and western United States. The abolition of the corn laws was a materialistic agitation for the abdication of King Cotton and the enthronement of King Wheat; but the change had strong moral implications.

From the days of Wilberforce and Clarkson in England and John Woolman and Elias Hicks in the United States, antislavery circles on both sides of the Atlantic had been boy-cotting slave-grown produce. In 1825 Clarkson was writing to Roberts Vaux of Philadelphia mentioning plans "to or-ganise a company to produce by free labour, manufacture and undersell commodities now produced entirely by slave labour." In 1838 an American Free Produce Association ran its own store in Philadelphia; and James Mott, husband of Lucretia, suffered great hardship by abandoning his dry goods business because it involved goods made from slave-grown cotton.[20] These were ineffectual gestures. Antislavery forces could count on more practical help from economic interests opposed to a slave economy. The abolition of slav-ery in the West Indies had owed much to the alliance be-tween evangelicals and the British East Indian interest which wished to break the West Indian sugar monopoly.[21] In 1839 the famous efforts of Nicholas Biddle and his Philadelphia bank to corner cotton on the Liverpool exchange, followed by an abrupt fall in American orders for Lancashire textiles as a result of the depression, led to a revival in Britain of the demand for new sources of raw cotton in India, and a new drive for British manufactures in the United States. Where-upon Joseph Pease and George Thompson, whose antennae were always sensitive to public opinion, organized a British India Society with the former object in view.

The British India Society was based upon the constitu-encies of Exeter Hall, and its membership consisted of the hard core of the antislavery forces. Two years later, when Cobden and his associates were organizing the National Anti-

Corn Law League, they persuaded Thompson to defer his Indian efforts and, instead, not only to devote to the cause of free trade his rhetorical gifts and standing with the free church clergy, but to bring with him to the League, lock, stock and barrel, the organization and membership of the British India Society, including the services of the editor of its journal.[22] By this astute political move Cobden acquired the support of organized antislavery forces, including the liveliest of its propagandists. He also inherited both the moral fervour and practical experience of the abolitionists. As Cobden testified, it was a few words from Joseph Sturge which

did more than anything to determine us to adopt for our principle, "the total and immediate repeal" of the Corn Law. . . . I remember how little the great majority were prepared for anything so strong and uncompromising . . . I believe it was our friend who, fresh from the experience of the Anti-Slavery struggle, pointed out the necessity of taking our stand on the rock of abstract truth and justice; and I must say we found it our rock of safety during our seven years' struggle.[23]

Thus the free trade movement drew strength from those same elements of opinion which most responded to the appeals of philanthropic radicalism. To quote Cobden again:

. . . and so far as the fervour and efficiency of our agitation has gone, it has eminently been a middle class agitation. We have carried it on by those means by which the middle-class usually carries on its movements. We have had our meetings of dissenting ministers; we have obtained the co-operation of the ladies; we have resorted to tea parties and taken those pacific means for carrying out our views which mark us rather as a middle-class set of agitators. We are no political body; we have refused to be bought by the Tories; we have kept aloof from the Whigs; and we will not join partnership with either Radicals or Chartists but we hold out our hand ready to give it to all who are willing to advocate the total and immediate repeal of the corn and provision laws.[24]

Harriet Martineau might have to remind her friend Maria Chapman in Boston that "your true alliance is with our League, as you all know through George Thompson. . . . The Anti-Corn Law League is, I do think, a noble body with a glorious function"; [25] but the possibilities of free trade for the antislavery cause were not lost upon American abolitionists, especially those who were seeking to transform moral exhortation into practical politics. Wendell Phillips greeted ecstatically the formation of the British India Society:

I am rejoiced to hear of your new movement in regard to India. It seals the fate of the slave system in America . . . You cannot imagine, my dear brother, the impulse this new development of England's power will give the Anti-slavery cause in America. It is just what we need to touch a class of men who seem almost out of the pale of religious influence . . . from India a voice comes clothed with the omnipotence of self-interest and the wisdom which might have been slighted from the pulpit will be to such men oracular from the market-place.[26]

Henry B. Stanton, with James G. Birney and Joshua Leavitt, secretary of the American and Foreign Anti-Slavery Society, were already considering the Anglo-American corollary to free cotton of free wheat, in their attempt to link the antislavery cause with the economic interest of the North and Northwest. In 1840 the need to find markets for her rich grain crops preoccupied Northwestern politicians as well as railway promoters with interests in the Mississippi Valley, like John Murray Forbes who was to combine railway propaganda with philanthropy by shipping midwestern grain to relieve the Irish Famine. An Ohio abolitionist, John Curtis, wrote a telling pamphlet in which he argued that "repeal of the corn laws would release the free states from their present commercial and consequent political vassalage to the Southern slave-holders." [27] Leavitt's proposal for free trade with Britain on the basis of an exchange of corn for manufactures was adopted as a major plank in the Liberty (antislavery) Party of 1840, and was the subject of Leavitt's widely read Memorial to Congress in the following year. The Liberty Party's Presidential candidate in 1840, James G. Birney, after attending the World Anti-Slavery Convention in London that summer, met Cobden in Manchester and tuned the Liberty Party's propaganda to that of the Anti-Corn Law League, of which he became a member. In 1841 the Liberty Party sent John Curtis to Manchester where he appeared at League meetings to testify to the abundance of Ohio's prairies and the moral force of free trade; and anti-corn law societies were even organized in America.[28]

Such proposals were ahead of their time. In the 1840's the new cotton-growing region of Texas once again reduced the price of raw cotton in Liverpool; the pressure for Indian supplies relaxed and the British India Society languished. King Cotton continued to hold sway. As for King Wheat, the happy coincidence of low wheat prices in America and high wheat prices in Britain, which had excited imaginations in 1839, proved temporary. It was another twenty years before American wheat began to flood the British market on the scale envisaged by the antislavery freetraders; [29] and by that time the slave interest was being choked, not by boycott, but by war. Nevertheless it was a grand design, worthy of the best elements among the abolitionists; and echoes of it persisted. In 1857 the New England Emigrant Aid Company attempted to recruit British emigrants for Kansas through the Cotton Supply Associations of Lancashire; [30] and Richard Cobden himself, with his American memories of 1835, invested the fortune subscribed for him in token of his free trade achievement, in the common stock of that "corn" railroad, the Illinois Central: an optimistic investment which caused him financial worry and an American visit on the eve of the Civil War.[31]

The abolition of the corn laws in 1846 was a great triumph for radical England. It represented a moral victory for a powerful insurgent class intent upon dismantling all the machinery of the establishment. The connection between free trade and other reforms is well expressed by Prentice in his contemporary history of the League:

From 1815 . . . (the) necessity (of Parliamentary reform) was mainly argued from the impolicy and the injustice of the corn laws; and the strong conviction of the impoverishing effects of the landowners' monopoly gave concentration to the energy which was put forth to obtain such a representation as would guarantee the adoption of free trade. Free trade, then, in the first place, peace, retrenchment, full religious liberty, the abolition of slavery in our colonies, wide constituencies in municipal elections, protection to the voter, and parliaments more frequently accountable to the people were the objects sought to be obtained . . . To this constant forward look to the practical, may be attributed the lead which Manchester took in the anti-corn law movement.[32]

There, indeed, spoke the voice of Manchester. For the effective attack on the establishment came from the great manufacturing middle class whose headquarters was to be found at Cottonopolis. It was this class with its Non-conformist business ethic, rather than Chartist *sans-culottes* or Bloomsbury intellectuals, who felt the closest affinities to the United States. These particular British people, intent on republicanizing British institutions, responded most sensitively to the American image. And their prophet was Richard Cobden.

Richard Cobden has moved in and out of these chapters, a leonine, intelligent fellow, a convinced opponent of the establishment, and, for all his posing as an armchair publicist, a clever practical politician. To come to grips with the affinities between England and America one must understand what he was trying to do.

Almost the first public act of this young calico-printer of Sabden and Manchester had been to write a revolutionary essay on the foreign policy of England. This book, published in 1835 with three editions in twelve months, embodies practically all the ideas which were to govern its author's career in national life.[33] Cobden's view of foreign policy is that of a new man, the Manchester man, the manufacturer and practitioner of political economy. Its object is international peace; but it is concerned not with the balance of power and dynastic conflict, but with an equilibrium in the material interests of common peoples. It is concerned not with "power politics" but with productivity; with raising living standards by spreading the benefits of the new industrialism through international trade. Its spirit is reminiscent of American liberal views towards foreign policy. Furthermore, its basis is an awareness of the Atlantic economy and of the lessons which must be learned from the young United States. It is, in fact, entitled *England, Ireland and America;* and though he wrote it just before he first visited the United States in 1835 a closer acquaintance only confirmed its conclusions.

Cobden opens by attacking the view that a cardinal point of British policy must be the buttressing of Turkey against Russia. Britain's true interests did not lie in involvement in the archaic and warlike affairs of the states and principalities of Europe and the Near East. "The middle and industrious classes of England can have no interest apart from the preservation of peace. The honours, the fame, the emoluments of war belong not to them; the battle-plain is the harvest-field of the aristocracy, watered with the blood of the people." [34] Nor did British interests lie in colonies; Britain's colonial policy had been, he thought, as sterile as Spain's and had involved formidable sacrifices of well-being for the sake of national pride.[35] Instead, Britain's true interest lay in free trade. Invoking the shade of Adam Smith, he stated in classic form the philosophy of free trade. This was the true foreign policy on moral as well as material grounds. "Commerce is the grand panacea which, like a beneficent medical discovery, will serve to inoculate with the healthy and saving taste for civilization all the nations of the world." [36] It was also the inexorable condition of the future.

If in the revolution of time and events a country should be found . . . whose cottons and woollens shall be cheaper than those of England . . . no human power, no fleets or armies, will prevent Manchester, Liverpool and Leeds from sharing the fate of their once proud predecessors in Holland, Italy and Phoenicia.[37]

This being so, Britain's true interest lay in the Atlantic.

It is a singular fact that whilst so much of the time and attention of our statesmen is devoted to the affairs of foreigners, and whilst our debates in Parliament and the columns of our newspapers are so frequently engrossed with the politics of petty states, such as Portugal, Belgium and Bavaria, little notice is taken of the country that ought, beyond all others, to engage the attention and even excite the apprehension of this commercial nation.

A considerable portion of our countrymen have not yet reconciled themselves to the belief that the American colonies of 1780 are now becoming a first-rate independent power . . . If these be told that the people of the U.S. constitute our largest and most valuable commercial connection—that the business we carry on with them is nearly twice as extensive as with any other people . . . they will express surprise; but then they will predict that no good will arise ultimately from trading with Yankee Republicans . . .

Yet it is to the industry, the economy and peaceful policy of America and not to the growth of Russia that our statesmen . . . ought to direct their anxious study; for it is by these, and not by the efforts of barbarian force, that the power and greatness of England are in danger of being superseded; yes, by the successful rivalry of America, shall we, in all probability, be placed second in the rank of nations.

The New World is destined to become the arbiter of the commercial policy in the old.[38]

For it was on trade that empires flourished and decayed. Cobden was ambivalent towards the United States; but he was more encouraged by her partnership than apprehensive about her competition. In American institutions lay the secret of productivity and progress. The prospects for trade with such a people were immense. In a vivid passage, he contrasted the actual prospects for trade and betterment with Turkey with the imaginary prospects of a Near East populated by Americans:

Constantinople, outrivalling New York, may be painted with a million of free citizens, as the focus of all the trade of eastern Europe. Let us conjure up the thousands of miles of railroads, carrying to the very extremities of this empire—not the sanguinary satrap, but—the merchandize and the busy traders of a free state; conveying, not the firman of a ferocious sultan . . . but millions of newspapers and letters, which stimulate the enterprise and excite the patriotism of an enlightened people. Let us imagine the Bosphorus and the sea of Marmora swarming with steamboats, issuing from the Dardanelles, to reanimate once more with life and fertility the hundred islands of the Archipelago; or conceive the rich shores of the Black Sea in the power of the New Englander and the Danube pouring down its produce from the plains of Moldavia and Wallachia, now subject to the plough of the hardy

Kentuckian. Let us . . . behold . . . hundreds of cities bursting from the tomb of ages, to recall religion and civilization to the spot from whence they first issued forth upon the world. Alas! that this should be only an illusion of the fancy! [39]

But America, for Cobden, was more than a natural trading partner and rival; she was the example to follow if Britain were to avoid being overtaken by her teeming productivity. The Americans were the best people, because their institutions were the most free: free commercial institutions which encouraged industry and enterprise; free religious institutions which encouraged morality:

If a word be said about the well-known religious and moral character of the Americans, [the] worthy [English] will stop you with the exclamation of, "How can there be religion or morality in a country that maintains no established church?" These don't read any traveller's tales except Moore, Trollope and Hall; [40]

free schools which fostered an educated people:

There is another peculiarity in the present attitude of the American people, as compared with our own, that is probably more calculated than all others to accelerate their progress towards a superior rank of civilization and power. We allude to the universality of education in that country . . . If knowledge be power, and if education give knowledge, then must the Americans inevitably become the most powerful people in the world; [41]

and finally the republican constitution which fostered non-intervention, economy, and peace in foreign affairs. For this Little Englander was a natural isolationist.

When Cobden returned home across the Atlantic in the fall of 1835, this self-appointed spokesman for the manufacturing classes, this bag-man, had a program for Britain in his carpetbag. For the England which he represented, if one may plagiarize President Eisenhower, "peace, prosperity, and

progress" were the ultimate objectives. In his eyes, the obstacle was the establishment: its irresponsible use of power
to promote warlike policies abroad, and to subdue the aspirations of the new, productive, beneficent middle classes at
home. The only way to overcome this obstacle was to dismantle the establishment, to dis-establish, so to speak, not
especially the Church of England—although full toleration
for Roman Catholics and Jews was to be one of Cobden's
aims—but all those English institutions which conserved an
inherited power in the hands of an outmoded ruling class.
The Reform Act had already made an initial breach in its
defences; but this must be exploited by a widely ranging
attack on social institutions, in which all the forces of light,
economic, religious, humanitarian, must be brought to bear.
There must be free schools to educate the new electorate and
the even wider electorate to come; there must be strict control
and retrenchment of the armed forces and civil service in the
interests of political economy and international peace; but
above all there must be an attack upon the establishment's
economic controls. Economic effort must be allowed to find
its own levels. "To keep the standard of living at its right
level, free access to the means of subsistence and the material of industry was the first essential." [42] This meant the
abolition of all controls over a free market for commerce,
capital and labor; and especially it meant the removal of all
obstructions to free trade. Much of the old mercantile system was in process of being dismantled piecemeal; but the
one great bulwark of the establishment in general and of the
landed aristocracy in particular, remained the corn laws. By
1838 it was clear to Cobden that an attack on these laws was
the central objective of his radical strategy. It was to this that
he gave priority; it was to this that he first of all devoted his
talents as a politician. The remedy for the old evils, for Cob-

den, was the agitation of public opinion. "There is no remedy," he had written of Tory resistance in *England, Ireland, and America,* "but in the wholesome exercise of the people's opinion in behalf of their own interests." [43] And so he exerted his political skill to canalize all possible support for his campaign: firstly, as he put it, "our mercantile and manufacturing classes as represented in the Chambers of Commerce [who] are after all the only power in the State possessed of wealth and political influence sufficient to counteract in some degree the feudal governing class of this country"; [44] and secondly, their allies in the middle and lower-middle class, the evangelical and free-church party with its concern for education, for peace, temperance, and antislavery.

From our point of view, the important thing is that Cobden was acting in an American frame of reference. As John Morley wrote of him: "The cardinal fact is the existence of the United States—its industrial competition and its democratic example. This has transformed the conditions of policy. This is what warns English statesmen to set their house in order." [45] When Cobden was elected to Parliament for Stockport in 1841 in the free trade cause he devoted an early speech to its American aspects. In pressing the point that the repeal of the corn laws would immensely encourage the exchange of food for manufactures with the United States, he developed the argument that the two countries were, after all, only sections of a single economy. Said Cobden:

Suppose now, that it were but the Thames instead of the Atlantic which separated the two countries, suppose that the people on one side were mechanics and artisans, capable by their industry of producing a vast supply of manufactures; and that the people on the other side were agriculturalists producing infinitely more than they could themselves consume of corn, pork and beef, fancy these two separate peoples anxious and willing to exchange with each other the produce of their common industries, and fancy a demon rising from the middle of the river . . . and holding in his hand an Act of Parliament, and saying, "You shall not supply each other's wants!" . . . Where was the difference between the Thames and the Atlantic? [46]

The Thames and the Atlantic. This was, indeed, a new trumpet call in foreign policy, although it must have sounded off-key to the ex-Foreign Secretary, Viscount Palmerston, and other Whig grandees whose inherited right it was to read the official dispatches. No wonder that Cobden and his colleague John Bright were known in Parliament as "the two Members for the United States." In California two giant redwoods were named, one for Cobden, one for Bright: a fitting monument to the American sympathies of the Manchester Man.

It now remains to consider the limits of this Atlantic connection in the early nineteenth century. In the first place, it was strictly an Anglo-American affair. In commerce, migration, and the carriage of political and philanthropic ideas, the Anglo-American element transcended any peripheral manifestations on the European continent. It is not possible to generalize, as continental scholars tend to do, about American cultural relations with western Europe as a whole, at any rate for this period. American relations with Britain, those Janus-faced islands on the Atlantic fringe of Europe, were of a different order of intimacy altogether.

Secondly, this connection involved particular groups of opinion in the two countries. In the United States it was limited to the Northern States. Despite King Cotton, the world we have described, in commerce, manufacture and migration, in political ideas, philanthropy, and education, if not exclusively in religion, was predominantly a northern world; and its motivating forces, dynamic, capitalistic, democratic, evangelistic, reformist, were essentially those which set it off from the South, and which ensured that in the great struggle between the two American sub-cultures, it should be the North which triumphed. The South had her own contacts with Britain; but they were with a Tory world, tenuous, ambivalent, sentimental, and waning in force. In the United Kingdom, this common Atlantic culture was shared characteristically, not with sectional groups, as in the United States, but with those particular classes, commercial, manufacturing, capitalist, artisan, intellectual, Dissenting, reformist, which represented a new order coming into being, and which were united in their efforts to reform the establishment. The spirit of these classes had something in common with that of the American revolutionaries who had grappled with the problem of a British establishment a generation before; and in their efforts, they were in part consciously attempting to republicanize Britain along American lines. This was also understood by their American sympathizers, like Henry B. Stanton, who wrote his book on British reformers

to induce candid Americans to make just discrimination in their estimate of "England and the English," and to draw distinctions between the privileged orders of that country and a small, but increasing, and even now powerful body of its people, who admire the free institutions of the United States and are laboring with heroic constancy and a zeal tempered with discretion, to secure for themselves and their fellow-subjects the rights and privileges enjoyed by trans-Atlantic republicans.[47]

Thirdly, even the groups which could be said to share this common outlook were hardly homogeneous in their opinions. Even in the northern United States its characteristic personalities might be at odds with the Atlantic connection in many important respects, from an inherited anglophobia to nativism and a belief in a high tariff against British manufactures. In Britain, even Richard Cobden, the arch-Americophile, feared American industrialization, spoke passionately against British emigration and, at the outbreak of the Civil War, was torn for a time between his admiration for Northern society and his concern for self-determination, peace, free trade, and cotton, which tempted him to cry "A plague o' both your houses!" The Atlantic connection concerned minority opinion and its ineffectiveness in moderating diplomatic friction between the two countries, from the War of 1812 to the Oregon crisis, needs no further comment. Yet its long-term influence was pervasive, as was shown by the role of a British opinion deriving from this connection during the American Civil War.

Lastly, this Atlantic connection flourished only for the limited time surveyed in these chapters. The Civil War marked an important stage in the economic evolution of the United States from "colonial" to "metropolitan" status, and after it, the concept of an Atlantic economy, based upon the complementary exchange of manufactures and raw materials, and the large-scale flow westward of labor and capital, becomes less valid. Henceforward, Americans turned inward, preoccupied with domestic markets and resources, and there rose to power a new social order based upon the wealth derived from industrialization. America's Atlantic connection related essentially to a mercantile economy which was powerfully affected by international trade and communication. Its intellectuals thought in English, not vernacular terms; its artisan radicals yearned to return to craft and landholding; its philanthropists were merchant princes, like Lewis Tappan, whose fortunes derived from overseas commerce, not industrialists, like John D. Rockefeller, who grew rich exploiting a primarily domestic market.

In Britain, also, the power of Atlantic ideas waned. The competition of an industrialized America profoundly disturbed capitalists. The America of the Gilded Age, extravagant and corrupt, confirmed the skeptics, and the Republic lost moral force. More important, during the second half of the century much of the radical program was achieved: successive reforms of Parliament, public education, a career open to talent, the universities open to Dissenters, and so on; but there was no revolution. The reformers did not succeed in dis-establishing institutions. The American model proved to be irrelevant to the special genius of British society. Even Cobden was aware of this. He wrote:

> they who argue in favour of a republic in lieu of a mixed monarchy, for Great Britain, are, we suspect, ignorant of the genius of their countrymen. Democracy forms no element in the materials of English character. An Englishman is, from his mother's womb, an aristocrat . . . The insatiable love of caste . . . pervades every degree from the highest to the lowest.[48]

The establishment was not dismantled, only reformed. Instead of republicanizing Britain on the basis of natural rights, the reformers only succeeded in broadening the spread of liberty, conceived as a privilege. The great commercial middle classes wrested a predominant share of power from the landed aristocracy and, under Gladstone, their Liberal Party set the tone of national politics. However, as had happened before and was to happen again in the mid-twentieth century, the establishment merely made suitable adjustments. Manufacturers bought landed estates and titles, married their daughters into the gentry, and sent their sons to Parliament; well-to-do professional men were absorbed into the aristocracy; the hierarchy of social power was not shattered, merely re-deployed. The appeal of America for British radicals lost its magic. From the 1890's, it was the Conservatives, taking their cue from people like Chamberlain, who made most of the United States, both as a potential ally in a threatening international world, and as an example of stable, conservative institutions for an England threatened with further constitutional reforms, including the abolition of that British Senate, the House of Lords. Moreover, when, in the twentieth century, a new force of outsiders, of non-conformists, gathered for another assault on the establishment, that force was no longer middle, but working class. Its ideology was socialist. The new image of America in England was not that of the republican, but that of the arch-capitalist; and the natural affinity between American democrats and the social democrats of the Labor Party was obscured.[49]

Yet these chapters may provide a clue to Anglo-American relations in the present. The most intimate connections between Englishmen and Americans are still among those who share in some degree the experience of uprooting. A newly-conservative United States can have only limited contact with a British establishment, for both are highly nationalist and introverted. A liberal America, however, in the dynamic tradition which made the United States the hope of the world in the early nineteenth century, would always strike a specially sympathetic response among those Englishmen whose inheritance derives from the reformist tradition with which we have been concerned. That inheritance is not wholly dissipated. Religious non-conformity is on the wane; but it would still be unwise to ignore the saying, attributed to Lord Palmerston, that "in the long run, English politics will follow the consciences of the Dissenters."

Notes

Chapter 1

1. *Times* (London), July 4, 1851.
2. For the authoritative exposition of this theme *see* Brinley Thomas, *Migration and Economic Growth: A Study of Great Britain and the Atlantic Economy* (Cambridge, 1954).
3. *See* F. Thistlethwaite, "Atlantic Partnership," *Economic History Review*, Vol. VII (1954).
4. Thomas, *op. cit.*, pp. 3-11.
5. For an able analysis of the American aspects of the Atlantic economy *see* Douglass C. North, "International Capital Flows and the Development of the American West;" *Journal of Economic History*, Vol. XVI (1957).
6. *See* Walter Prescott Webb, *The Great Frontier* (London, 1953), Chap. 1, and *passim*.
7. For the use of the term "Metropolis," *see* Webb, *op. cit., especially* pp. 8-13.
8. *See* Ragnar Nurkse, "International Investment Today in the Light of Nineteenth Century Experience," *The Economic Journal*, Vol. LXIV (1954).
9. North, *loc. cit.*
10. G. R. Taylor, *The Transportation Revolution, 1815–1860* (New York, 1951), Appendix A, Tables 10 and 13; *see also* L. H. Jenks, *The Migration of British Capital to 1875* (London, 1927), p. 67.
11. R. G. Albion, *The Rise of New York Port, 1815–1860* (New York, 1939), pp. 57, 98.
12. *Ibid.*, p. 99; Taylor, *op. cit.*, p. 186.
13. R. G. Albion, *op. cit.*, p. 99.
14. *Ibid.*, pp. 57-59.
15. Herbert Heaton, "The American Trade, 1793–1815," in C. Northcote Parkinson (ed.), *Trade Winds, A Study of British Overseas Trade During the French Wars, 1793–1813* (London, 1948), pp. 204-06.
16. *Parliamentary Papers, 1830–31*, X, 47: Statement of the Shipping Employed in the United Kingdom, 1814–1820.
17. *See* N. S. Buck, *The Organization of Anglo-American Trade, 1800–1850* (New Haven, 1925), *passim*.
18. Herbert Heaton, "Yorkshire Cloth Traders in the United States, 1770–

1840," in Thoresby Society *Publications,* misc. for 1941, Vol. XXXVII, Pt. 3; *see also* Herbert Heaton, "The Industrial Immigrant in the United States, 1783–1812," American Philosophical Society *Proceedings,* Vol. 95, No. 5 (1951).

19. See Albion, *op. cit., passim.*

20. Jeremiah Thompson still awaits a biographer; for the Thompson family and its business connections *see* Herbert Heaton, *Yorkshire Cloth Traders;* C. P. Wright, *The Origins and Early Years of the Transatlantic Packet Ships of New York, 1817–1835* (unpublished dissertation, Harvard University Library, 1932); entry for Jeremiah Thompson by C. P. Wright in *Dictionary of American Biography;* R. G. Albion, *op. cit.,* and *Square Riggers on Schedule* (Princeton, 1938).

21. Albion, *New York Port,* p. 38.

22. The masters of both ships were entertained by the British community at the annual St. George's Day Dinner, and New Yorkers demonstrated that affectionate interest, which has persisted, in the comings and goings of British liners. Anon., *A History of the St. George's Society of New York from 1770 to 1913* (New York, 1913), p. 45. Isambard Kingdom Brunel thought of his revolutionary *Great Western* as the means of projecting across the Atlantic his great empire of steam, the Great Western Railway, and of reviving the fortunes of the port of Bristol. L. T. C. Rolt: *Isambard Kingdom Brunel* (London, 1957), p. 191.

23. Wright, *op. cit.,* and *Dictionary of American Biography;* Albion, *New York Port,* p. 114.

24. Wright, *op. cit.;* Albion, *New York Port,* p. 114.

25. Albion, *New York Port,* p. 100.

26. Heaton, *Yorkshire Cloth Traders,* pp. 272-74.

27. Albion, *New York Port,* p. 238.

28. Moses Yale Beach, *Wealth and Wealthy Citizens of New York City,* 1842–1855 annual, varying titles (1846 volume). This figure includes the Irish when in linen or dry goods, and second-generation British when still connected with the parental firm. For about half of the Beach list no particulars are given so that the above figure is likely to be an under-estimate. To be worth $100,000 was Beach's definition of a rich man.

29. The information here summarized was compiled chiefly from Beach, *op. cit.; A History of St. George's Society of New York from 1770 to 1913* (New York, 1913); G. A. Morrison, *History of the St. Andrew's Society of the State of New York, 1756–1906* (New York, 1906); cf. *An Historical Catalogue of the St. Andrew's Society, of Philadelphia, with Biographical Sketches of Deceased Members* (Philadelphia, 1907); E. S. Gardner (ed.), *The First Two Hundred Years of the St. Andrew's Society of Philadelphia* (Philadelphia, 1947).

30. Heaton, *op. cit.,* p. 265.

31. *History of St. George's Society of New York,* p. 135.

32. Beach, *op. cit.;* Morrison, *op. cit.* Stewart was a multimillionaire by the time of the Civil War; Albion, "Commercial Fortunes in New York," *New York History,* XVI (1935), p. 167.

33. The career of Benjamin Marshall is as important for Atlantic history as that of his partner Jeremiah Thompson. Attracted by the possibilities of cotton manufacturing behind the tariff, he abandoned his merchant business in New York in 1825 and with his brother established a group of cotton mills at Troy which proved exceptionally successful. He did much to improve the town of Troy, developing its water power at great profit himself, and founding churches, schools, and an infirmary to which he left much of his fortune. The career of this early Victorian merchant, millowner, and philanthropist, transplanted across the Atlantic, deserves further research. *See* entry by C. P. Wright in *Dictionary of American Biography*; Nathan Crosby, *Annual Obituary Notices of Eminent Persons Who Have Died in the United States for 1858* (Boston, 1859), pp. 208-11; Beach, *op. cit.*, n.p.; H. J. Carman and A. B. Gold, *The Rise of the Factory System*, in A. C. Flick, ed., *History of the State of New York* (New York, 1934), VI, 195-96; Albion, *New York Port, passim*.

34. For James Boorman, of the British firm of Boorman and Johnston, *see* Beach, *op. cit.*, n.p.; *History of St. George's Society*, n.p.; Anon., *Portrait Gallery of the Chamber of Commerce of the State of New York* (New York, 1890); Albion, *New York Port*, p. 238. Boorman's career foreshadows that of John S. Kennedy, whose progress from salesman for the Mossend Iron and Coal Co. to his extensive activities on behalf of British railway investors in the United States falls largely outside the period; *see* Morrison, *op. cit.*, pp. 123-30. For Cartlidge *see* John Ramsey, *American Potters and Pottery* (New York, 1939), pp. 111-12; E. A. Barber, *The Pottery and Porcelain of the United States* (New York, 1909), pp. 163-64; Cartlidge was only one of several pottery importers turned manufacturer.

35. *History of St. George's Society*, n.p.; Beach, *op. cit.*, n.p.

36. *The Albion, A Weekly Journal of News, Politics and Literature* (New York, 1822–1875); *The Anglo-American* (New York, 1843-47).

37. Such societies also flourished in Philadelphia. Niblo, the "incomparable" impresario and restaurateur, was British-born.

38. *History of the St. George's Society of New York, passim*; Robert Ernst, *Immigrant Life in New York City, 1825–1863* (New York, 1949), pp. 42-43, 82-98, 126-27, 178-79; Albion, *New York Port*, p. 238.

39. Thomas L. Nichols, *Forty Years of American Life* (London, 1864), II, 79.

40. For the structure of Anglo-American trade *see* N. S. Buck, *op cit., passim*. The American Chamber of Commerce in Liverpool was founded by an American, James Maury, merchant and first United States Consul of that port. His son Matthew, who was educated at Eton, returned to New York to establish an American branch of the family firm in 1822. *Portrait Gallery of the Chamber of Commerce of New York*, pp. 66-67.

41. The greater part advanced to cotton dealers. Margaret G. Myers, *The New York Money Market* (New York, 1931), I, 66.

42. For the Brown family *see* J. C. Brown: *A Hundred Years of Merchant Banking: A History of Brown Bros. and Co.* (1909); *Brown Brothers and Company: Experiences of a Century, 1818–1918* (Philadelphia, 1919); entry

under Sir William Brown in Dictionary of National Biography; *Portrait Gallery of New York Chamber of Commerce*, pp. 238-40.

43. For George Peabody *see* Muriel Hidy, *George Peabody, Merchant and Financier, 1829-1854* (unpublished dissertation, Radcliffe College, Cambridge, Mass., 1939): Peabody is one of the few Americans with entries in the *Dictionary of National Biography*, and the *Dictionary of American Biography*.

44. *See* Ralph W. Hidy, *The House of Baring in American Trade and Finance* (Cambridge, Mass., 1949).

45. Myers, *op. cit.*, I, 29.

46. Ralph W. Hidy, *op. cit.*, p. 29.

47. N. A. McNall, *An Agricultural History of the Genesee Valley, 1790-1860* (Philadelphia, 1952), pp. 14, 23; *see also* Helen I. Cowen, "Charles Williamson, Genesee Promoter—Friend of Anglo-American Rapprochement"; Rochester Historical Society *Publications*, Vol. XIX (1941).

48. Joseph Schafer, *The Wisconsin Lead Region* (Madison, 1932), pp. 148-54, which contains a useful estimate of the long term profitability of this investment. *See also* the same author's "Lands Across the Sea," *Wisconsin Magazine of History*, Vol. XIII (1929-30).

49. Margaret Myers, *op. cit.*, I, 36.

50. Charles J. Bullock, John H. Williams and Rufus S. Tucker, "The Balance of Trade of the United States," *Review of Economic Statistics*, Preliminary I (1919), Appendix B.

51. Myers, *op. cit.*, I, 36.

52. N. S. B. Gras and Miss H M. Larson, editors' introduction, Hidy, *op. cit.*, pp. xvii-xviii.

53. J. M. Swank, *History of the Manufacture of Iron in All Ages and Particularly in the United States* (2nd ed., Philadelphia, 1892), pp. 256, 434, 441.

54. Thomas, *op. cit.*, pp. 159-63.

55. M. L. Hansen, *The Atlantic Migration, 1607-1860* (Cambridge, Mass., 1945), pp. 194-95.

56. Thomas, *op. cit.*, Chap. 2.

57. U. S. Department of Commerce, *Historical Statistics of the United States, 1789-1945* (Washington, 1949), Series B. 306, p. 33; J. B. Brebner, *North Atlantic Triangle: The Interplay of Canada, the United States and Great Britain* (New Haven, 1945), p. 109 n.

58. U. S. Census for 1860; U. S. Department of Commerce, *Historical Statistics of the United States, 1789-1945* (Washington, 1949), Series B. 281, p. 32; all emigration figures must be treated with caution, in view of the notorious incompleteness of the emigration statistics for the period, owing to the absence of figures for returning emigrants, and for re-emigration from Canada, the inaccuracy of the declared destination, the difficulty of distinguishing Irish from other British emigrants, and other causes; for contemporary discussions *see* Jesse Chickering, *Immigration into the United States* (1848), pp. 42-50; W. J. Bromwell, *History of Immigration* (1856) *passim*.

59. For the Birkbeck settlement *see* Chap. 2, pp. 48-51.

60. In the considerable literature relating to British emigrants on the frontier, the accounts of these two families are singled out as being particularly illuminating; Rebecca Burlend, *A True Picture of Emigration*, M. M. Quaife (ed.) (Chicago, 1936), is a classic narrative of survival against the characteristic hazards of the back country; John Muir, *The Story of My Boyhood and Youth* (1913) contains a vivid picture of wild life and farming practice in the Wisconsin wilderness.

61. M. M. Quaife (ed.), "An English Settler in Pioneer Wisconsin: The Letters of Edwin Bottomley, 1842–1850." State Historical Society of Wisconsin, *Collections*, Vol. XXV (1918).

62. For the Potter's Emigration Society, which was supported by the Potters' Union of the Five Towns of Staffordshire, *see* Harold Owen, *The Staffordshire Potter* (London, 1901), Chaps. 4 and 5; Grant Foreman, "The Settlement of English Potters in Wisconsin," *Wisconsin Magazine of History*, Vol. XXI (1938); for the Liverpool Temperance Emigration Society scheme at Gorstville, Wisconsin, *see* Chap. 3 below, p. 94 n.; for the Iowa community *see* Jacob Van der Zee, *The British In Iowa* (Iowa City, 1922), p. 28; W. S. Shepperson, "Industrial Emigration in Early Victorian Britain," *Journal of Economic History*, Vol. XIII (1953).

63. J. D. B. De Bow, *Statistical View of the United States, Being a Compendium of the Seventh Census*, Table cxx, p. 117.

64. For an admirable essay on the social assimilation of different ethnic groups, including the British-born, *see* Joseph Schafer, "The Wisconsin Lead Region," *Wisconsin Domesday Book, General Studies* (Madison, 1927 onwards), III, 235-49; this series of volumes, which treats the early history of Wisconsin county by county, provides valuable evidence, both quantitative and qualitative, of the fortunes of sizeable groups of British immigrants, both farmers and miners.

65. Smith's business career began with Lord and Taylor in New York and then was associated with the big New York wholesale house of Ira Smith. Joseph Schafer, "The Winnebago-Horicon Basin," *Wisconsin Domesday Book, General Studies*, IV, 180-81; *National Cyclopaedia of American Biography*; information provided by Miss Alice Smith, Wisconsin Historical Society, Madison, Wis.

66. Bayard Still, *Milwaukee, The History of a City* (1948), pp. 58-60; L. B. Krueger, *History of Commercial Banking in Wisconsin* (Madison, 1933), *passim*; J. D. Butler, "Alexander Mitchell, the Financier," *Wisconsin Historical Collections*, Vol. XI (1895); Joseph Schafer, "Four Wisconsin Counties, Prairie and Forest," *Wisconsin Domesday Book, General Studies*, II, 78-79; articles for Smith and Mitchell by Louise Kellogg in *Dictionary of American Biography*; Frances W. Gregory and Irene D. Neu, "The American Industrial Elite in the 1870's: Their Social Origins," in William Miller (ed.), *Men in Business* (Cambridge, Mass., 1952), p. 198.

67. De Bow, *op. cit.*, Table cxx, p. 117.

68. T. W. Page, "The Distribution of Immigrants in the United States before 1870," *Journal of Political Economy*, Vol. XX (1912).

69. Ernst, *op. cit.*, pp. 43-44, 72, 74-75, Tables 1, 2.

70. R. T. Berthoff, *British Immigrants in Industrial America* (Cambridge, Mass., 1953), p. 82.

71. Ernst, *op. cit.*, pp. 126, 148, 155, 156.

72. For the Cornish *see especially* L. A. Copeland, "The Cornish in Southwest Wisconsin," *Wisconsin Historical Collections*, Vol. XIV (1898); James E. Jopling, "Cornish Miners of the Upper Peninsula," *Michigan History Magazine*, Vol. XII (1928); J. Schafer, *The Wisconsin Lead Region, passim;* John Sirjamaki, "The People of the Mesabi Range," *Minnesota History*, Vol. XXVII (1946); Berthoff, *op. cit.*, pp. 58-61.

73. Andrew Roy, *A History of the Coal Miners of the United States* (Columbus, 1903) *passim;* E. A. Wieck, *The American Miners' Association* (New York, 1940), pp. 77-80; Berthoff, *op. cit.*, pp. 47-54. *See below,* p. 57 n.

74. For the pottery industry *see especially* U. S. Department of Commerce, Bureau of Foreign and Domestic Commerce, Misc. Series No. 21: *The Pottery Industry* (Washington, 1915); Ohio Bureau of Labor Statistics, *19th Report* (1895); John Ramsey, *op. cit.;* E. A. Barber, *op. cit.; History of the Upper Ohio Valley with Historical Account of Columbian County, Ohio* (Madison, Wis., 1891); from these and other sources the author has compiled skeleton biographies of a hundred British potters who emigrated to the United States before 1873; *see* Frank Thistlethwaite, "The British Migrant Technician in the Atlantic Economy: The Case of the Potter," paper delivered before the European Association for American Studies, Paris, Sept. 1957.

75. Swank, *op. cit.*, pp. 309-10, 358-62, 369-70, 383-88, 450-55; Berthoff, *op cit.*, pp. 62-65.

76. The following authorities are especially useful in tracing the British element in American textiles: J. Montgomery, *The Cotton Manufacture of the United States of America Contrasted and Compared With That of Great Britain* (Glasgow, 1840); George S. White, *Memoir of Samuel Slater* (Philadelphia, 1836); Samuel Batchelder, *Introduction and Early Progress of the Cotton Manufacture in the United States* (Boston, 1863); J. L. Bishop, *A History of American Manufactures from 1608–1860* (Philadelphia, 1868); Royal C. Taft, *Some Notes on the Introduction of the Woollen Manufacture into the United States* (1882); Caroline F. Ware, *The Early New England Cotton Manufacture* (Boston, 1931); Arthur H. Cole, *The American Wool Manufacture* (Cambridge, Mass., 1926); Herbert Heaton, "The Industrial Immigrant in the United States, 1783–1812," American Philosophical Society, *Proceedings*, Vol. 95, No. 5 (1951).

77. Berthoff, *op. cit.*, Chap. 3; for Philadelphia *see* "Testimony of witnesses accompanying the Report of the Committee . . . to investigate the employment of children in Manufactories," *Pennsylvania Senate Journal* (Session of 1837–38), II, 278-359; the author is indebted to Mr. William A. Sullivan for calling attention to this source.

78. Charles Cowley, "The Foreign Colonies of Lowell," The Old Residents' Historical Association *Contributions*, Vol. II (Lowell, 1880).

79. Henry H. Earl, *A Centennial History of Fall River* (New York, 1877); Thomas Russell Smith, *The Cotton Textile Industry of Fall River, Mas-*

sachusetts, A Study of Industrial Localization (New York, 1944); Sylvia Chace Lintner, *A Social History of Fall River 1859–1879* (unpublished thesis, Radcliffe College Library); Robert K. Lamb, *The Development of Entrepreneurship in Fall River 1815–1859* (unpublished thesis, Harvard Library, 1935).

80. *See below*, Chap. 2, p. 57 and n.

81. Although it is to be suspected that the Irish referred to in the standard works were usually those who had learned their trade during a sojourn in Lancashire before making their final migration.

82. *See* Lamb, *op. cit.*

83. *See* L. H. Jenks, *The Migration of British Capital to 1874*, (New York, 1927), Chaps. 3 and 4. The best analysis of American fluctuations as they affected Anglo-American economic relations is R. C. O. Matthew: *A Study in Trade Cycle History: Economic Fluctuations in Great Britain, 1837-1843* (Cambridge, 1954), Chap. 5.

84. M. T. Copeland, *The Cotton Manufacturing Industry of the United States* (Cambridge, Mass., 1912), pp. 9-11; Montgomery, *op. cit., passim.*

85. Dyer's career is of some significance for this study. Apart from his agency for American inventions, he was a joint founder of the *North-American Review* in 1815 and of the *Manchester Guardian* in 1821 and helped to establish the Manchester Mechanics' Institution. An abolitionist and a free trader, he was prominent in the public life of Manchester, and earned an entry in the *Dictionary of National Biography. See* W. H. G. Armytage, "Some Aspects of American Influence on British Education." Address delivered to Section L (education) at the Sheffield Meeting of the British Association, 1956.

86. H. H. Earl, *op. cit.*, p. 57.

87. *See* Dorothy R. Adler, *British Investment in American Railways, 1834–1898* (unpublished dissertation, Cambridge University Library, 1958), Chapter 2.

Chapter 2

1. G. D. Lillibridge, *Beacon of Freedom: The Impact of American Democracy upon Great Britain 1830–1870* (Philadelphia, 1954).

2. The influence of Dissent will be treated separately in subsequent chapters.

3. *Carpenter's Political Letters and Pamphlets,* "A Political Digest," December 23, 1830; quoted in Lillibridge, *op. cit.*, p. 24.

4. G. L. Nesbitt, *Benthamite Reviewing; The First Twelve Years of The Westminster Review, 1824–36* (New York, 1934), p. 48.

5. Richard Cobden, *England, Ireland and America* (Edinburgh, 1836), p. 33.

6. *Charter,* October 20, 1839; quoted in Lillibridge, *op. cit.*, p. 49.

7. For an analysis of this literature *see* J. L. Mesick, *English Travellers in*

184 *Notes*

America 1785–1835 (New York, 1922) and M. Berger, *The British Traveller in America, 1836–1860* (New York, 1943).

8. James Stuart, *Three Years in North America* (Edinburgh, 1833); J. S.
Buckingham, *America, Historical, Statistic and Descriptive* (London, 1841–
43); E. S. Abdy, *A Journal of A Residence in the United States of North
America* (London, 1835); Harriet Martineau, *Society in America* (London,
1837) and *Retrospect of Western Travel* (London, 1838); Joseph Sturge,
A Visit to the United States in 1841 (London, 1842); George Combe,
Notes on the United States (Edinburgh, 1841).

9. For Cooper *see* Dumas Malone, *The Public Life of Thomas Cooper, 1783–
1839* (New Haven, 1926), for Priestley *see* J. T. Rutt (ed.), *The Life and
Correspondence of Joseph Priestley* (London, 1831); Anne Holt, *A Life
of Joseph Priestley* (London, 1931); Mary Cathryne Park, "Joseph Priestley
and the Problem of Pantisocracy," Delaware County Institute of Science,
Publications, Vol. X (Philadelphia, 1947); E. F. Smith, *Priestley in America, 1794–1804* (Philadelphia, 1920).

10. Joseph Priestley, "Of the Constitution of the United States," *Lectures on
History and General Policy* (new edition, ed. J. T. Rutt, London, 1826),
Appendix, pp. 576-77.

11. Thomas Pears and his wife, Sarah. Sarah, daughter of the Rev. Thomas
Fyshe-Palmer (the Unitarian associate of Priestley who had been trans-
ported to Botany Bay for sedition in 1794) had arrived in America with
her mother in the same year. Thomas Pears had been a partner in a
Pittsburgh glassworks with Thomas Bakewell, whose uncle Benjamin was
one of the original advance party of the Priestley venture. The other
partner in the glassworks was John James Audubon who married Thomas
Bakewell's sister. *See* T. C. Pears, "New Harmony: An Adventure in Happiness: the Papers of Thomas and Sarah Pears," Indiana Historical Society *Publications*, Vol. XI (1933); Park, *op. cit.; Dictionary of National
Biography* entry for Thomas Fyshe-Palmer, *Dictionary of American Biography* entry for Audubon; *see also* C. D. Snedeker (ed.), "The Diaries of
Donald Macdonald, 1824–26," Indiana Historical Society *Publications*,
Vol. XIV (1942).

12. *See* Park, *op. cit.*, p. 31.

13. C. B. Johnson, *Letters from the British Settlement in Pennsylvania* (Philadelphia, 1819) *passim;* Emily C. Blackman, *History of Susquehanna
County, Pennsylvania* (Philadelphia, 1873), pp. 377, 454-56, and especially
a letter by Mrs. William Turner to the *New York American*, dated Susquehanna County, September 3, 1821, *ibid.*, pp. 376-77. Johnson, like Birkbeck, was accused by disillusioned settlers of looking at the American
backwoods through rose-tinted spectacles: "With a little care . . . the
most delightful groves could be left, interspersed with the fields. . . .
What a treat it would be to a landscape gardener in England to have
such cutting and carving! What could not Price, Gilpin, Repton or
Capability Brown have given for such materials to work with . . ."; Johnson, *op. cit.*, p. 57.

14. Of the enormous bibliography of works relating to the English Prairie,

the following have been found the most useful: Morris Birkbeck, *Notes on a Journey in America from the Coast of Virginia to the Territory of Illinois* (London, 1817) and *Letters from Illinois* (London, 1818); George Flower, "History of the English Settlement in Edwards County, Illinois," Chicago Historical Society *Collections*, Vol. I (1882); George Flower, *The Errors of Emigrants* (London, 1841); F. A. Ogg (ed.), *Personal Narrative by Elias Pym Fordham* (Cleveland, 1906); Jay Monaghan (ed.), "From England to Illinois in 1821: The Journal of William Hall," Illinois State Historical Society *Journal*, Vol. XXXIX (1951), Parts I and II; J. Woods, *Two Years' Residence in the Settlement on the English Prairie* (London, 1822); J. E. Inglehart, "The Coming of the English to Indiana in 1817 and Their Hoosier Neighbours," *Indiana Magazine of History*, Vol. XV (1919); C. W. Alvord, *Governor Edward Coles* (Springfield, 1920); Walter Colyer, "Address on the Fordhams and La Serres of the English Settlement in Edwards County," Illinois State Historical Society *Proceedings* (1911); E. E. Sparks (ed.), *The English Settlement in the Illinois* (1907); S. J. Buck, *Illinois in 1818* (1917).

15. *See* Alvord, *op. cit.*, pp. 141-61.
16. Morris Birkbeck, Oration, July 4, 1822, Wanborough, Illinois; *Niles Register*, October 5, 1822, XXIII, 73-75.
17. *See* H. B. Fearon, *Sketches of America* (2nd edition, London, 1919), p. 423. Like Fearon, William Faux was sent to prospect in America, and especially to the Birkbeck settlement, on behalf of a group of intending immigrants, who appear to have been farmers from a similar district of East Anglia to that of the Flowers and Fordhams; William Faux, *Memorable Days in America, Being a Journal of a Tour of the United States* (London, 1823), list of subscribers, pp. xi-xvi. For Cobbett's letters to Birkbeck *see* William Cobbett, *A Year's Residence in America* (Abbey Classics edition n. d.), pp. 235-69.
18. Frances Wright, *Views of Society and Manners in America* (London, 1821); the best account of Nashoba and of Frances Wright is in A. J. G. Perkins and Theresa Wolfson, *Frances Wright, Free Inquirer* (New York, 1939); W. R. Waterman, *Frances Wright* (New York, 1924).
19. Robert Owen, *A Discourse of a New System of Society* (Washington, 1825).
20. Of the enormous literature on New Harmony the following are most useful: Robert Dale Owen, *Threading My Way* (London, 1874); J. W. Hiatt (ed.), "Diary of William Owen, 1824-25," Indiana Historical Society *Publications*, Vol. IV (1906); C. D. Snedeker, *op. cit.*; T. C. Pears, *op. cit.*; R. W. Leopold, *Robert Dale Owen* (Cambridge, Mass., 1940); A. E. Bestor, *Backwoods Utopias* (Philadelphia, 1950).
21. Joseph Dorfman, *The Economic Mind in American Civilization* (New York, 1946), II, 638.
22. The materials collected by Macdonald were later used by John Humphrey Noyes in writing his *History of American Socialisms*.
23. *See especially:* A. E. Bestor, "Education and Reform at New Harmony: Correspondence of William Maclure and Marie Duclos Fretageot," Indiana

Historical Society *Publications*, Vol. XV (1948); Harvey L. Carter, "William Maclure," *Indiana Magazine of History*, Vol. XXXI (1935); W. H. G. Armytage, "William Maclure 1763–1840: A British Interpretation," *Indiana Magazine of History*, Vol. XLVII (1951); C. A. Browne, "Some Relations of the New Harmony Movement to the History of Science in America," *The Scientific Monthly* (June, 1936); Walter B. Hendrickson, "David Dale Owen and Indiana's First Geological Survey," *Indiana Magazine of History*, Vol. XXXVI (1935).

24. The Fruitlands Community, of Harvard (village), Massachusetts traces its origins to an Englishman, James Pierrepont Greaves, who was a disciple of Pestalozzi and at the time of his death in 1842 was in process of converting his school at Ham Common in Surrey into a fully-fledged communitarian experiment. Bronson Alcott persuaded Charles Lane, Greaves's lieutenant, to transfer the experiment to the United States, Lane providing the finance. Like many such experiments, Fruitlands soon broke up as a result of discordant personalities. Frank Sanborn, *Bronson Alcott at Alcott House, England and Fruitlands, New England, 1824–44* (1908); O. Shephard, *Pedler's Progress* (Boston, 1937), pp. 326, 345; A. E. Bestor, *op. cit.*, p. 140 considers Alcott House at Ham Common "the one communitarian experiment of 1840's in the British Isles that exerted a direct influence upon the American movement." For the British Icarians *see* "The British Section of Icarian Communists," *Bulletin of the International Institute for Social History*, No. 2 (1937), and W. S. Shepperson, *loc. cit.*; Cabet was influenced in London by Owen who may have been responsible for the choice of Texas.

25. C. E. Persons, "The Early History of Factory Legislation in Massachusetts," Part 1 of *Labor Laws and Their Enforcement, with Special Reference to Massachusetts* (New York, 1911), pp. 13, 14, 16; Robert Ernst, *Immigrant Life in New York City, 1825–1863* (New York, 1949), pp. 99, 182; John R. Commons: *Documentary History of American Industrial Society* (Cleveland, Ohio, 1910–11), V, 23.

26. Commons, *op. cit.*, Vol. IV, supplement, pp. 29, 116.

27. Persons, *op. cit.*, pp. 24-25, and *passim; Massachusetts Bureau of Statistics of Labor, Eleventh Annual Report* (January, 1880), pp. 6-9; H. M. Fenner, *History of Fall River* (1911), p. 141; P. S. Foner, *History of the Labor Movement in the United States* (New York, 1947), pp. 204-07; G. J. Holyoake, *A History of Co-operation* (London, 1875-9), II, 455-56.

28. Andrew Roy, *A History of the Coal Miners of the United States* (Columbus, 1903), pp. 59-72; E. A. Wieck: *The American Miners' Association* (New York, 1940), pp. 77-80; from these two sources the author has compiled biographical sketches of some twenty-seven early British miners, many of whom became union leaders and mine bosses, and a few State mine inspectors.

29. John R. Commons, *et al.*, *History of Labor in the United States* (New York, 1918), II, 25 n. J. R. Commons (ed.), *Documentary History of American Industrial Society* (Cleveland, 1910–11), VIII, 249-62.

30. Louis H. Arky, "The Mechanics' Union of Trade Associations and the

Formation of the Philadelphia Workingmen's Movement," *Pennsylvania Magazine of History and Biography*, Vol. LXXVI (1952).

31. J. F. Bray, *Labour's Wrongs and Labour's Remedy* (Leeds, 1839); Bray was born in the United States, to a theatrical family, and lived there until he was twelve. See articles on Bray by M. Joliffe, *International Review for Social History*, Vol. IV (1939) and by H. J. Carr, *Economica*, Vol. VII (new series, 1940).

32. W. R. Waterman, *op. cit.*, pp. 144-47; Leopold, *op. cit.*, p. 57.

33. *The Beacon*, which was the most persistent, was published between 1836 and 1844.

34. J. Q. Adams, *Memoirs* (Philadelphia, 1874-7), XI, 408-09.

35. *The Beacon*, Vol. II, No. 14 (February 3, 1838).

36. For Offen and Vale *see* Lewis Masquerier, *Sociology* (New York, 1877), pp. 105-06, 123-24; and *The Beacon, passim*.

37. Horace Traubel, *With Walt Whitman in Camden* (New York, 1906-14), III, 140.

38. *The Radical Reformer and Working Man's Advocate*, 19 numbers, published weekly between June 13, 1835 and October 17, 1835.

39. Thomas Brothers, *The United States As They Are: Not as They Are Generally Described; Being a Cure for Radicalism* (London, 1840).

40. *Southern Star*, May 24, 1840, quoted in Lillibridge, *op. cit.*, pp. 43-44.

41. Julius West, *History of the Chartist Movement* (Boston, 1920), pp. 191, 253.

42. Henry Ashworth, *A Tour in the United States, Cuba and Canada* (London, 1861), pp. 173-74.

43. *Red Republican*, June 22, 1850, quoted in H. Pelling, *America and the British Left, from Bright to Bevan* (London, 1956), p. 58; George Holyoake, *Bygones Worth Remembering* (London, 1905), I, 11-12.

44. R. T. Berthoff, *British Immigrants in Industrial America* (Cambridge, Mass., 1953), p. 104.

45. J. McCabe, *Life and Letters of G. J. Holyoake* (London, 1908), II, 109.

46. Masquerier, *op. cit.*, p. 106.

47. He was also concerned with an abortive English colony in Montana. W. J. Linton, *Memories* (London, 1895), p. 212.

48. John Campbell, *A Theory of Equality or the Way to Make Every Man Act Honestly* (Philadelphia, 1848); *see* his letters to the *New York Tribune*, August 6, November 29, December 13, 1850; W. Brotherhead, *Forty Years Among The Old Booksellers of Philadelphia* (Philadelphia, 1891).

49. *Working Man's Advocate*, August 24, November 30, December 4, 1844; Persons, *op. cit.*, pp. 42, 58, 85; Norman Ware, *The Industrial Worker, 1840-60* (Boston, 1924), pp. 139-41; Foner, *op. cit.*, p. 202.

50. For Devyr's career *see* his spirited autobiographical account: *The Odd Book of the Nineteenth Century, or 'Chivalry' in Modern Days, a Personal Record of Reform—Chiefly Land Reform for the Last Fifty Years* (New York, 1882); *see also Working Man's Advocate*, April 6, May 11, 18, 25; June 1, 8; July 20; November 16, 1844; G. J. Holyoake, *Sixty Years of an Agitator's Life* (London, 1892), I, 178; and *Among the Americans*,

and *A Stranger in America* (Chicago, 1881), p. 133; Masquerier, *op. cit.*, p. 123.

51. Devyr, *op. cit.*, pp. 134, 161, passages transposed.
52. *Ibid.*, p. 43.
53. Henry Christman, *Tin Horns and Calico: A Decisive Episode in the Emergence of Democracy* (New York, 1945).
54. For the exchange of intelligence between these American and British radical sheets *see Working Man's Advocate* (2nd Series, 1844-45, New York), and *Young America* (1845-50, irregular); for British knowledge of American land reformers *see Working Man's Advocate*, e.g., issues of May 25; June 1, 8; August 17, 31, 1844; these journals are saturated with "News from the Rotton Monarchies," by which was largely meant Great Britain. *See also* H. S. Zahler, *Eastern Workingmen and National Land Policy, 1829-62* (New York, 1941), pp. 76-79.
55. *Working Man's Advocate*, July 20, 1844.
56. *Ibid.*, January 4, 1845.
57. For the career of George Henry Evans *see:* Frederick W. Evans, *Autobiography of a Shaker* (New York, 1869), pp. 12-41; F. Byrdsall, *The History of the Loco-foco or Equal Rights Party* (New York, 1842); Zahler, *op. cit.*; Ware, *op. cit.*, pp. 183-84; Commons, *Documentary History*, Vol. VII, Introduction; *Working Man's Advocate*, March 23, 1844; October 12, 1844.
58. Masquerier, *op. cit.*, p. 95.
59. Holt, *op. cit.*, p. 201.
60. Frances Wright, Address on Tom Paine, Cincinnati, Ohio, February 29, 1838; printed in *The Beacon*, March 17, 1838.
61. Paul Palmer, "Benthamism in England and America," *American Political Science Review*, Vol. XXXV (1941).

Chapter 3

1. For the eighteenth century background to these connections *see* Michael Kraus, *The Atlantic Civilization. Eighteenth Century Origins* (Ithaca, N. Y., 1949).
2. Bishop Horsley, *Freedom of the Press* (1793), p. 131, quoted in Anthony Lincoln, *Some Political and Social Ideas of English Dissent, 1783-1800* (Cambridge, 1938), p. 256.
3. Robert Southey, "On the Rise and Progress of Popular Disaffection" in *Essays, Moral and Political* (1832), II, 73; quoted in *ibid.*, p. 26.
4. *Edinburgh Review*, April, 1838.
5. For the Unitarians in England *see especially* E. M. Wilbur, *A History of Unitarianism in Transylvania, England and America* (Cambridge, Mass.,

1952), Chaps. XV-XIX; H. McLachlan, *The Unitarian Movement in the Religious Life of England* (London, 1934) and R. V. Holt, *The Unitarian Contribution to Social Progress in England* (London, 1938). For American Unitarianism *see* Wilbur, *op. cit.,* Chaps. XX-XXIII.

6. Her brother James, the leading Unitarian divine, was, however, a conservative in social values.

7. It included John Vaughan, of a prominent English Unitarian family, and Ralph Eddowes, an ex-Member of Parliament and pupil of Priestley at Warrington; their church was built with British aid in 1813; Wilbur, *op. cit.,* pp. 397-98.

8. Wilbur, *op. cit.,* pp. 394-96.

9. *Ibid.,* p. 371.

10. The firm of William Rathbone & Co. is said to have received, in 1784, the first cargo of American cotton, which was consigned to a Unitarian, Strutt of Belper. William Rathbone, Sr. was at that time still a Quaker.

11. *See* Joseph Sturge, *A Visit to the United States* (London, 1841); J. J. Gurney, *A Journey in North America. Described in Familiar Letters to Amelia Opie* (Norwich, 1841); the minutes of London Yearly Meeting and Meeting for Sufferings strikingly reveal the extent of this transatlantic traffic (Friends' House Library, London). The relation of trade with Quakerly philanthropy is illustrated by the Thompson-Cropper connection. (*See* Chap. 1, p. 15). James Cropper, of Cropper, Benson and Co., Liverpool was a powerful antislavery and peace advocate, and father-in-law of Joseph Sturge. Jeremiah Thompson was secretary of a Manumission Society in New York and a trustee of the New York Free School Society; he also entertained Robert Owen and Frances Wright in New York and contributed to both New Harmony and Nashoba. Heaton, *Cloth Traders, op. cit.,* p. 259; Perkins and Wolfson, *op. cit.,* p. 138; Diary of Donald Macdonald, *loc. cit.,* pp. 180-4; Diary of David Owen, *loc. cit.,* p. 24.

12. Minutes of London Meeting for Sufferings, May 6, 1836.

13. The report of the deputation consisting of William Forster, George Stacey, Josiah Forster and John Allen, is contained in Minutes of London Yearly Meeting for 1846.

14. H. Codman, *Narrative of a Visit to England* (1836); H. Humphrey, *Great Britain, France and Belgium: A Short Tour* (1838); Andrew Reed and James Matheson, *Narrative of the Visit to the American Churches, by the Deputation from the Congregational Union of England and Wales* (London, 1835); Gilbert H. Barnes and D. L. Dumond (Eds.), *Letters of T. D. Weld, A. Grimké Weld and S. Grimké, 1822-44* (New York, 1934), I, 338, note; W. P. and F. J. Garrison, *The Life and Times of William Lloyd Garrison* (New York, 1885), I, 479-81.

15. An initial sum of six thousand pounds was raised for the founding of Kenyon in 1826. G. F. Smythe, *Kenyon College, Its First Century; see also Chase Papers* (Kenyon College); N. S. Wheaton, *Journal of a Residence During Several Months in London* (1830).

16. A generous contribution came from the Lenox circle of New York. James

Lenox, son of the Scots immigrant merchant, acted as an American coun-
seller for Thomas Chalmers and the Free Church. George Shepperson,
"Thomas Chalmers, the Free Church of Scotland and the South," *Journal
of Southern History*, Vol. XVII (1951).

17. *See* E. R. Taylor, *Methodism and Politics, 1791–1851* (Cambridge, 1935);
E. Halévy, *A History of the English People in 1815* (London, 1924),
pp. 359-74.

18. Halévy, *op. cit.*, pp. 378-84.

19. F. Warre Cornish, *The English Church in the 19th Century* (London,
1910), I, 33.

20. Halévy, *op. cit.*, p. 374. Even the peculiar tenets of the Society of Friends
were overwhelmed by evangelicalism which, in America, brought about
the split between orthodox and Hicksite meetings.

21. The importance of these German origins must not be overlooked, especially that of the University of Halle where, at the beginning of the eighteenth century a full pattern of evangelistic benevolence—practical charity,
education, tract-printing, music, and missionary work—was already fully
established, and of the Moravians whose missionary communities in Pennsylvania so impressed both Wesley and Whitefield. I am indebted to a
paper by Mr. Deitmar Rothermund of the University of Pennsylvania
for bringing out the full Anglo-American significance of the German
influence.

22. A. E. Payne, "The Evangelical Revival and the Beginnings of the Modern
Missionary Movement," *Congregational Quarterly*, Vol. XXI (1943). When
Edwards was ejected from his Northampton living in 1750 Erskine suggested a living in Scotland and other Scots friends offered financial support. A. L. Drummond, *The Story of American Protestantism* (Edinburgh, 1949), p. 124.

23. Drummond, *op. cit.*, p. 181.

24. Whitefield, who altogether made seven American journeys, died in America and was buried in the Old South Presbyterian Church, Newburyport,
Massachusetts.

25. For the Welsh revivalists *see* R. Ayton, *Voyage round Great Britain* (London, 1815), II, 71; quoted in Halévy, *op. cit.*, p. 367.

26. Timothy L. Smith, *Revivalism and Social Reform in Mid-Nineteenth
Century America* (New York, 1957); *see also* entries for individual evangelists in the *Dictionary of American Biography*.

27. Arthur, whose original mission was to raise money for Irish Methodists,
became an influential evangelist, especially through his book, *The Tongue
of Fire* (1856). Smith, *op. cit.*, p. 122.

28. It is worth noting that the heady atmosphere of the New World which,
as we have seen, made a land reformer of the British immigrant, George
Henry Evans, turned his brother Frederick towards the Shaker discipline
and a career as a prominent Elder; *see* Frederick W. Evans, *op. cit.* For
the Oliphants, *see* Margaret Oliphant, *Memoir of the Life of Laurence
Oliphant* (London, 1891); H. W. Schneider and G. Lawton, *A Prophet
and a Pilgrim; Being the Incredible History of Thomas Lake Harris and*

Laurence Oliphant (New York, 1942). Oliphant married Rosamund, daughter of Robert Dale Owen, as his second wife.

29. Reed and Matheson, *op. cit.*, II, 300.

30. Robert E. Spiller, *The American in England During the First Half Century of Independence* (London, 1926), p. 245.

31. George S. White, *Memoir of Samuel Slater* (Philadelphia, 1835), p. 107. Jedediah Strutt was a Unitarian.

32. The Presidents of the Missionary Societies of New York and Connecticut were Foreign Directors of the London Missionary Society as early as 1798; London Missionary Society, *Annual Reports* for 1798, 1799; Eugene Stock, *History of the Church Missionary Society* (London, 1899), I, 155.

33. William Canton, *History of the British and Foreign Bible Society* (London, 1904–10), I, 241-50.

34. *Ibid.*, pp. 126, 241-50.

35. R. E. Spiller, *op. cit.*, p. 209.

36. However, E. S. Abdy believed that Sing Sing was an imitation of the Maison de Force at Ghent, and the Eastern States Penitentiary at Philadelphia, of Glasgow. E. S. Abdy, *A Journal of a Residence in the United States of North America* (London, 1835), I, 17.

37. Harriet Martineau, *Society in America*, III, 179-80; *Autobiography, with memorials by Maria Weston Chapman* (London, 1877), I, 269.

38. Most reformers among the British travellers, especially Abdy, Sturge, Gurney and Miss Martineau, made a point of visiting penitentiaries, along with deaf and dumb and insane asylums.

39. Samuel Tuke, *Description of the Retreat . . . near York* (York, 1813); Dr. Benjamin Rush was improving upon the methods of Pinel and other Europeans in his treatment of mental disease at the Philadelphia Hospital from 1783 onwards. Alice Felt Tyler, *Freedom's Ferment* (Minneapolis, 1944), pp. 301-02. The treatment of the deaf and dumb is a similar story in which the outstanding figure is the American Samuel Gridley Howe, whose success in educating a deaf-blind girl created a sensation in Britain as well as America in the 1840's; Harold Schwartz, *Samuel Gridley Howe, Social Reformer* (Cambridge, Mass., 1956), pp. 88-90.

40. Letter of O'Connell to Joseph Pease, December 13, 1839; A. M. Stoddart, *Elizabeth Pease Nichol* (London, 1899), p. 102.

41. L. Sears, *Wendell Phillips: Orator and Agitator* (New York, 1909), frontispiece.

42. This organization, and especially its centralized character, may have owed a good deal to Methodist example; *see* Raymond English, "George Thompson and the Climax of Philanthropic Radicalism, 1830–1842" (unpublished dissertation).

43. For the multifarious philanthropy of Arthur Tappan *see* the list of his good causes in E. P. Southall, "Arthur Tappan and the Anti-Slavery Movement," *Journal of Negro History*, Vol. XV (1930).

44. C. A. Ingraham, "The Birth at Moreau of Temperance Reformation," New York State Historical Association, *Proceedings*, 1906, VI, 115-33; J. A. Krout, *The Origins of Prohibition* (New York, 1925), pp. 77-8, 129-30,

and map opposite p. 130; Gilbert H. Barnes, *The Anti-Slavery Impulse* (New York, 1933); W. R. Cross, *The Burnt-Over District* (Ithaca, New York, 1950).

45. Krout, *op. cit.*, p. 129.

46. John Dunlop, *The Extent and Remedy of National Intemperance*; Samuel Couling, *History of the Temperance Movement in Great Britain and Ireland* (London, 1862), pp. 34-35.

47. Couling, *op. cit.*, pp. 42-43.

48. *Ibid.*, pp. 44-46.

49. This concern for emigrants, fused with the Utopian dream of an alcohol-free community in the American wilderness, led in 1843 to the formation in Liverpool, under the sponsorship, among others, of Lawrence Heyworth, M. P., a prominent temperance leader, of a British Temperance Emigration Society, the object of which was the establishment of a British emigrant community at Gorstville, Wisconsin. The story of this community, which ultimately withered away, may be read in William Kittle, *History of the Township and Village of Mazomanie* (Madison, 1900); *see also British Emigration Society Papers* (Wisconsin State Historical Society, Madison, Wis.); Joseph Schafer, *The Wisconsin Lead Region*, pp. 208-09.

50. John Bartholomew Gough's visits to Britain, in 1853, 1857 and 1878 were, for him, a return to his native land which he had left as a child emigrant. *See* J. B. Gough, *Autobiography* (London, 1879); and *Sunlight and Shadows* (London, 1881), which gives a vivid impression of the London poor in the fifties; Carlos Martyn, *John B. Gough* (New York, 1894).

51. Money which he lost as a result of the collapse of American banking stocks in 1839. J. S. Buckingham, *The Coming Era of Practical Reform* (London, 1853), pp. 39-56; *see also* R. E. Turner, *James Silk, Buckingham, 1780–1855, A Social Biography* (London, 1934).

52. Couling, *op. cit.*, pp. 182-86; J. S. Buckingham, *op. cit.*, pp. 523-32; Krout, *op. cit.*, p. 217.

53. The word, spoken by one "Dickie" Turner, a working man, was the result, according to some accounts, of a stutter, of others, of a quirk of the Lancashire dialect. There is, however, a Scottish claim for the term's etymology. Couling, *op. cit.*, p. 59; J. S. Buckingham, *op. cit.*, p. 438; Krout, *op. cit.*, p. 158n. Joseph Livesey, *Two American Villages, Peterboro' and Auburn, the One Reformed, the Other Unreformed: The Result of a Careful Visitation* (Preston, 1836), suggests American influence.

54. Couling, *op. cit.*, p. 92.

55. Krout, *op. cit.*, p. 158-63.

56. Couling, *op. cit.*, pp. 112-19. The controversy turned on whether or not the signer should be committed to denying intoxicants to others and should be allowed them for medicinal and sacramental purposes.

57. Joseph Sturge, *op. cit.*, pp. 101, 104.

58. Couling, *op. cit.*, p. 225; *see* entry for Neal Dow, *Dictionary of American Biography*.

59. Merle Curti, *The American Peace Crusade 1815–1860* (Durham, N. C., 1929), p. 146.

60. A. Prentice, *A Tour in the United States, with Two Lectures on Emigration* (Manchester, 1849), pp. 129-30. *See also* Frederick Douglass' sentiments in P. S. Foner (ed.), *The Life and Writings of Frederick Douglass* (2 Vols., New York, 1950), *passim*.
61. Noah Worcester, *A Solemn Review of the Custom of War* (Greenfield, Mass., 1817); Curti, *op. cit.*, pp. 12-15; the London society was more properly called the London Society for the Promotion of Permanent and Universal Peace.
62. Curti, *op. cit.*, p. 38.
63. *Ibid.*
64. Stephen Hobhouse, *Joseph Sturge, His Life and Work* (London, 1919), pp. 121-22. American Friends were much less prominent than English Friends in the peace, as in the antislavery, movements. *See* Curti, *op. cit.*, pp. 16-17.
65. Curti, *op. cit.*, p. 79.
66. A characteristic Garrisonian gesture, similar to that which led to the disruption of the American Anti-Slavery Society in the same year. *See below*, p. 117; Curti, *op. cit.*, pp. 81-82.
67. *Ibid.*, pp. 175, 176, 182.
68. *Ibid.*, pp. 114-117, 159. For the Address of the National Charter Association to "The Working Classes of America," *see* William Lovett, *Life and Struggles* (London, 1879), pp. 312-19.
69. Curti, *op. cit.*, p. 153. Burritt's lieutenant in Britain was Edmund Fry, son of Elizabeth Fry; he also received support from the Anti-Corn Law Leaguers and especially from its President, George Wilson. For the connection between the peace and anti-corn law movements *see below*, p. 155.
70. Curti, *op. cit.*, pp. 157-65. For "universal reform" *see below*, pp. 117, 153-157. Burritt was to return to England in 1865 on being appointed by President Lincoln United States Consul in Birmingham.
71. *See* William Jay, *War and Peace: the Evils of the First and a Plan to Preserve the Last* (1842).
72. Sturge, *op. cit.*, pp. 57, 129, 140, Appendix F; Henry Richard (ed.), *Memoirs of Joseph Sturge* (London, 1864), pp. 351-53; Bayard Tuckerman, *William Jay and the Constitutional Movement for the Abolition of Slavery* (London, 1893), p. 130; Hobhouse, *op. cit.*, p. 156.
73. It obtained seventy-nine votes; Hansard's *Parliamentary Debates*, CVI, 1849, Volume V of Session, pp. 54-122; Curti, *op. cit.*, pp. 190-93.
74. *Ibid.*, pp. 194-95.

Chapter 4

1. *See* Joseph Sturge, *op. cit.*, Preface.
2. *See especially*, Anthony Benezet, *A Caution and Warning to Great Britain and Her Colonies on the Calamitous State of Enslaved Negroes* (1766),

and *An Historical Account of Guinea* (1771); A. T. Gary, "Political and Economic Relations of English and American Quakers, 1750–1785," p. 190 (unpublished dissertation in the Library, Friends' House, London, with an excellent chapter on anti-slavery activities); Thomas E. Drake, *Quakers and Slavery in America* (New Haven, 1952), *passim;* Rufus M. Jones, *The Later Period of Quakerism* (London, 1921), I, 318-19; F. J. Klingberg, *The Anti-Slavery Movement in England: A Study in English Humanitarianism* (New Haven, 1926), p. 75.

3. J. G. Birney to Lewis Tappan, July 27, 1840: D. L. Dumond (ed.), *The Letters of J. G. Birney, 1831–57* (New York, 1938), II, 585; the phrase seems to have been a cliché: "The Quakers are the 'bone and muscle' of the English anti-slavery interests"; John Keep, in England to raise funds for Oberlin College, to Gerrit Smith, London, Nov. 13, 1839; Calendar of Gerrit Smith Papers at Syracuse University (1941), p. 122, No. 453.

4. Letter from the editor of the *Glasgow Courier* to editor of *Royal Gazette* of Jamaica, reprinted in the *Anti-Slavery Reporter,* August 31, 1826.

5. Oratio oblique rendered into direct speech; General Meeting of the Anti-Slavery Society, December 21, 1825; *Anti-Slavery Reporter,* VIII, 1.

6. Raymond English, "George Thompson and the Climax of Philanthropic Radicalism, 1830–1842" (unpublished dissertation), p. 77. I am much indebted to Mr. English, of Kenyon College, Ohio, for the loan of a copy of this dissertation, which is the authoritative source.

7. Angelina Weld to Anna R. Frost, August 18, 1829: *Weld-Grimké Letters,* II, 789.

8. Klingberg, *op. cit.,* p. 304.

9. *Ibid.,* p. 273.

10. *Ibid.,* pp. 273-75.

11. English, *op. cit.,* p. 409.

12. John Emory (ed.), *The Works of John Wesley* (New York, 1825), VII, 237.

13. *See* E. L. Fox, *The American Colonization Society, 1817–1840* (Baltimore, 1919); the idea was anticipated by British evangelicals who in 1787 organized the colony of Sierra Leone for the few British slaves freed by the court decisions of 1772 and 1778 and Negroes carried off by the British army in the American Revolution. Klingberg, *op. cit.,* pp. 106 ff; Drake, *op. cit.,* pp. 122-23.

14. Frederick Douglas, Emancipation Day speech 1857; Foner, *op. cit.,* II, 428, 434.

15. Foner, *op. cit.,* II, 326, 427-28, 433-34, 502-18; Sears, *op. cit.,* pp. 130, 176; Garrisons, *op. cit.,* I, 450.

16. *See* letter of invitation to the inaugurating convention by Tappan, Leavitt and Wright, October 29, 1833; *Weld-Grimké Letters,* I, 117. Tuckerman, *op. cit.,* pp. 45, 49.

17. For Garrison in London *see* Garrisons, *op. cit.,* I, Chap. 11.

18. Phillips' address unveiling the statue of Harriet Martineau in Old South Church, Boston, 1883.

19. Garrisons, *op. cit.,* II, 230.

20. English, *op. cit.,* p. 303.

21. Foner, *op. cit.*, I, 226-27, 237-38.
22. *See* Max Berger, "American Slavery as seen by English Visitors, 1836–1860," *Journal of Negro History*, Vol. XXX. It is worth noting that E. S. Abdy, whose visit to the United States overlapped those of Harriet Martineau and George Thompson, had a long interview with W. E. Channing which was instrumental in converting Channing to the anti-slavery cause; Abdy, *op. cit.*, III, 217-40; Harriet Martineau, "The Martyr Age in the United States," *Westminster Review* (December, 1838) reprinted as *The Martyr Age in America, with an appeal on Behalf of the Oberlin Institute in Aid of the Abolition of Slavery* (London, 1840), p. 14.
23. Tuckerman, *op. cit.*, p. 54; A. B. Hart, *Slavery and Abolition* (New York, 1906), p. 236.
24. For George Thompson in America *see especially* Garrisons, *op. cit.*, Vol. I; *Weld-Grimké Letters*, Vol. I; *Birney Letters*, Vol. I; English, *op. cit., passim*.
25. Presidential Message to Congress, Dec. 7, 1835; quoted in Garrisons, *op. cit.*, II, 73.
26. Hart, *op. cit.*, p. 184; cf. Martineau, *op. cit.*, p. 15; Sears, *op. cit.*, p. 63; *Liberator*, VI, 49; C. C. Burleigh, *The Reception of George Thompson in Great Britain* (London, 1836); English, *op. cit.*, p. 409.
27. Hart, *op. cit.*, p. 273.
28. For Stuart *see* Barnes, *Anti-Slavery Impulse*, p. 14 and Chap. 3, esp. pp. 33, 35, 37 and n.; *Weld-Grimké Letters*, I, 48, 74 and n.; D. M. Ludlum, *Social Ferment in Vermont* (New York, 1939), p. 159; Garrisons, *op. cit., passim;* Theodore Weld's first son was named Charles Stuart Weld, just as William Lloyd Garrison and George Thompson named sons after each other.
29. Martineau, *The Martyr Age in America; see also* Martineau, *Autobiography*, II, 23-24.
30. Richard, *op. cit.*, pp. 204-05; for the American orientation of the new society *see* British and Foreign Anti-Slavery Society, *First Annual Report* (London, 1840), pp. 5-7.
31. The Sturge-Tappan correspondence is published in A. H. Abel and Frank J. Klingberg (eds.), *A Side-light on Anglo-American Relations, 1839–1858, furnished by the Correspondence of Lewis Tappan and Others with the British and Foreign Anti-Slavery Society* (Lancaster, Pa., 1927).
32. For accounts of these conventions *see: Proceedings of the General Anti-Slavery Convention Called by the Committee of the British and Foreign Anti-Slavery Society and Held in London . . . June 12-23, 1840* (London, 1841); and *Proceedings of the Convention . . . Held June 13-20, 1843* (London, 1843).
33. It was prompted by a suggestion in an article in the New York *Emancipator*, March 21, 1838; *Proceedings* (1840), p. 20.
34. *Proceedings* (1840), p. 3.
35. Phillips to Thompson, 1839; *Speeches and Letters by Wendell Phillips* (Boston, 1891), pp. 7-9.

36. *Proceedings* (1840), p. 125.
37. Especially that of the Baptists F. A. Cox and J. Hoby in 1835; Garrisons, I, 479-81; *see above*, p. 81.
38. *Proceedings* (1840), pp. 59-76.
39. Published, London, 1841. Clarkson said he was led to write it by a voice in a dream crying "You have not done all your work; there is America." E. L. Griggs, *Thomas Clarkson, the Friend of Slaves* (London, 1936), pp. 182-84.
40. British and Foreign Anti-Slavery Society, *2nd Annual Report*, 1841.
41. British and Foreign Anti-Slavery Society *8th Annual Report*, 1847, pp. 21-24.
42. See British and Foreign Anti-Slavery Society *Annual Reports, 6th*, 1845, p. 18; *7th*, 1846, pp. 31-32; George Shepperson, "Thomas Chalmers, the Free Church of Scotland and the South," *Journal of Southern History*, Vol. XVII (1951).
43. Epistle to North Carolina, May 24, 1837.
44. *See* Sturge's letter to John Greenleaf Whittier sounding him out on the question, Richard, *op. cit.*, p. 224; *also ibid.*, p. 238; Sturge's parting shot as he left America was an *Address to Members of the Religious Society of Friends in the United States of America* (New York, 1841); for his comments on American Friends *see also A Visit*, pp. 30, 98, 127; Elizabeth Pease had contributed *The Society of Friends in the United States and Their Views of the Slavery Question* in 1838, an indictment in which she was aided by American Quakerly informants; A. M. Stoddart, *Elizabeth Pease Nichol* (London, 1899), pp. 109-10; C. S. Abdy was also critical of American Friends; Abdy, *op. cit.*, I, 388; III, 187-201, 319.
45. S. J. May, *Some Recollections of the Anti-Slavery Conflict* (Boston, 1869), pp. 335-44.
46. Proslavery sentiment in the Protestant Episcopal Church prevented the publication of an American edition of Samuel Wilberforce's *History of the Protestant Episcopal Church in America*. Its hostile references to slavery were printed as a separate pamphlet by William Jay in 1846; Tuckerman, *op. cit.*, pp. 133-34.
47. *Proceedings* (1840), p. 126.
48. Martineau, *Autobiography*, p. 57.
49. Nathaniel P. Rogers to his wife, July 28, 1840, quoted in R. S. Arthur, *Nathaniel Peabody Rogers, 1794–1846, New Hampshire Abolitionist*, Chap. 1, p. 2 (unpublished thesis, Haverford College Library, Pennsylvania; I am indebted to Mr. Arthur for the loan of a copy of this dissertation). Rogers characteristically added of the English: "they have none of [prejudice against color] but abound in it against low birth and poverty." Lewis Tappan's judgement of English character is hardly more flattering. In 1846, commenting on an English Quaker delegation to Indiana he wrote: "When Englishmen come here and see how much abolitionists are hated or despised, they recoil from us, as the losing of caste to an Englishman is a very sad affair." Tappan to Birney, April 29, 1846; *Birney Letters*, II, 1012.
50. B. Quarles, *Frederick Douglass* (Washington, 1948), p. 52; for Douglass's

British visits and connections, especially with Julia Griffiths, *see* Foner, *op. cit., passim;* Douglass said that he "breathed freer on British soil than elsewhere. . . . When I go to church, I am met by no upturned nose and scornful lip to tell me 'we don't allow niggers here.' " Douglass to Garrison, Jan. 1, 1846, Foner, *op. cit.,* I, 127-28; J. H. Franklin, *From Slavery to Freedom* (New York, 1952), p. 249, lists, in all, eleven Negro abolitionists who visited Europe.

51. Barnes, *The Anti-Slavery Impulse,* p. 169-70; for a version more favorable to Garrison *see* Garrisons, *op. cit.,* II, 346-47.

52. *See* Able and Klingberg, *op. cit.* Introduction, *passim;* the nickname was used by Joshua Leavitt, *Birney Letters,* II, 603.

53. Sears, *op. cit.,* p. 118.

54. *See* British and Foreign Anti-Slavery Society, *Annual Reports,* esp. 2nd (1841) and 3rd (1842).

55. Klingberg, *op. cit.,* p. 306; Klingberg, "Harriet Beecher Stowe and Social Reform in England," *American Historical Review,* Vol. XLIII (1938); Professor Klingberg makes the point that the characteristic British contribution to the destruction of slavery was the blue book, that of America, the popular novel. Among the mementoes presented to Mrs. Stowe during her visit to England in 1853 was a silver inkstand with Religion, Bible in hand, giving liberty to the slave as a white man knocks the shackles from his feet.

56. *See especially,* D. Jordan and E. J. Pratt, *Europe and the American Civil War* (London, 1931); Wilbur D. Jones, "The British Conservatives and the American Civil War," *American Historical Review,* Vol. LVIII (1953); R. Harrison, "British Labour and the Confederacy: A Note on the Southern Sympathies of some British working class journals and leaders during the American Civil War," *International Review of Social History,* Vol. II (1957).

57. For general background to the women's movement *see especially,* I. B. O'Malley, *Women in Subjection: A Study of Englishwomen Before 1832* (London, 1933); E. C. Stanton, S. B. Anthony and M. S. Gage (eds.), *A History of Woman Suffrage* (New York, 1881–1902), Vols. I, II; Helen Blackburn, *Record of Women's Suffrage* (London, 1902); W. Lyon Blease, *The Emancipation of English Women* (London, 1913).

58. Harriet Martineau, *Autobiography, With a Memorial by Maria Weston Chapman* (London, 1877); Lydia Maria Child, *Letters from New York* (London, 1843); Lydia Child also wrote a *History of the Condition of Women in Various Ages and Nations* (Boston, 1832).

59. *See,* for example, Harriet Martineau's forthright statement in *Society in America,* pp. 199-207; compare, however, *Autobiography,* I, 399-41.

60. For Hannah More's influence on feminine manners in the United States *see* M. Curti, *The Growth of American Thought* (New York, 1943), p. 197.

61. Dorothea Dix, a Unitarian, lived for eighteen months with the William Rathbones at Greenbank, Liverpool, in 1837–38; entry for Dorothea Dix in *Dictionary of American Biography.*

62. Curti, *The American Peace Crusade*, pp. 23-24, 31, 154, 160-61.

63. Krout, *op. cit.*, pp. 215-17; for Margaret Bright Lucas *see* entry in the *Dictionary of National Biography*.

64. *Liberator*, November 7, 1835.

65. Elizabeth Heyrick, *Immediate, Not Gradual Emancipation; or an Inquiry into the Shortest, Safest and Most Effectual Means of Getting Rid of West Indian Slavery* (London, 1824). According to Sturge this pamphlet, which had an American edition the same year, was responsible for converting William Jay to the antislavery cause. Sturge, *op. cit.*, p. 56.

66. L. M. Child to E. Carpenter, September 6, 1838; Child, *Letters*, p. 23.

67. *History of Woman Suffrage*, I, 334 n.; Maria Chapman was educated in England; Martineau, *Martyr Age*, pp. 18-19.

68. Abdy, *op. cit.*, p. 210.

69. Julia Griffiths's father, of Newcastle-on-Tyne, was a close friend of William Wilberforce; for her connections with Douglass *see* Foner, *op. cit.*, I, pp. 87-92; Quarles, *op. cit.*, pp. 88, 92, 107; *North Star* had a number of English subscribers.

70. Garrisons, *op. cit.*, I, p. 337.

71. *Weld-Grimké Letters*, I, 350 n., Angelina Grimké, *A Letter to the Christian Women of the Slave States of America* (New York, 1835).

72. English, *op. cit.*, p. 312.

73. Carlos Martyn, *Wendell Phillips: The Agitator* (New York, 1890), p. 117.

74. A. D. Hallowell, *James and Lucretia Mott* (Boston, 1884), p. 115.

75. *Ibid.*, pp. 122-23; W. B. C. and A. C. Wyman, *Elizabeth Buffum Chase: Her Life and Its Environment* (Boston, 1914), I, 103.

76. *Weld-Grimké Letters*, I, 414.

77. Pastoral Letter of the General Association of Massachusetts, 1837, quoted in *History of Woman Suffrage*, I, 81-82.

78. Martineau, *Martyr Age*, p. 37.

79. *History of Woman Suffrage*, I, 89; *see also* Elizabeth Buffum Chase, *Anti-Slavery Reminiscences* (Central Falls, R. I., 1891), concluding words.

80. Maria Weston Chapman, *Right and Wrong in Boston* (Boston, 1837), p. 73; Martineau, *Martyr Age*, p. 40.

81. It is worth noting that the Garrisonians also forced the admission of women to the annual convention of the American Peace Society in Boston in 1838; Curti, *Peace Crusade*, pp. 81-82.

82. *Weld-Grimké Letters*, I, 834.

83. *History of Woman Suffrage*, I, 50-62; Sears, *op. cit.*, pp. 79-82; Martyn, *op. cit.*, p. 133; T. Stanton and H. S. Blatch, *Elizabeth Cady Stanton as Revealed in Her Letters, Diary and Reminiscences* (New York, 1922), is a most lively, indeed, racy contemporary account; F. B. Tolles, *Slavery and The Woman Question: Lucretia Mott's Diary, 1840* (London, 1952). A large group portrait of the Convention, painted by Benjamin Haydon, hangs in the National Portrait Gallery, London.

84. The admission of women was still "repugnant to the English mind," in

Elihu Burritt's words, at the International Peace Convention held in London in 1851; Curti, *op. cit.*, p. 136.

85. N. P. Rogers, *The Sphere of Woman: The Envoy from Free Hearts to the Free* (Pawtucket, 1840), quoted in Arthur, *op. cit.*, Chap. v, p. 7.

86. Stanton and Blatch, *op. cit.*, I, 79-80; Elizabeth Cady Stanton had already earned the disapproval of Birney on shipboard crossing the Atlantic. He considered it unladylike of her to play "tig" on deck, to be hoisted to the masthead in a chair and to call her husband "Henry" in public. *Ibid.*, I, 69-70.

87. *History of Woman Suffrage*, I, 423; William Howitt thought the real issue centred round Lucretia Mott who, as a Hicksite Friend, was suspect by orthodox London Quakers. This certainly exacerbated the matter. *See* Howitt to Lucretia Mott, June 27, 1840, quoted in *History of Woman Suffrage*, I, 435-37.

88. Martyn, *op. cit.*, p. 134; *History of Woman Suffrage*, I, 432-33.

89. Garrisons, *op. cit.*, II, p. 353; *History of Woman Suffrage*, I, p. 437.

90. *History of Woman Suffrage*, I, 421.

91. *Ibid.*, p. 418.

92. *Ibid.*, pp. 375 ff.

93. Stoddart, *op. cit.*, *Weld-Grimké Letters, passim; History of Woman Suffrage*, I, 438; Blackburn, *op. cit.*, pp. 15, 95-100.

94. Address of the Sheffield Political Association to the Women of England, drawn up at a meeting of the Sheffield Female Political Association, held at the Democratic Temperance Hotel, Sheffield, on Feb. 26, 1851. This association appears to have been formed during the Chartist agitation. R. Strachey, *The Cause*, (London, 1928), p. 43; Blackburn, *op. cit.*, p. 19; *History of Woman Suffrage*, I, 226, 438.

95. I. B. O'Malley, *Florence Nightingale, 1820–1856; A Study of her Life Down to the End of the Crimean War* (London, 1931), pp. 72-73 and *Women in Subjection*, p. 350; Strachey, *op. cit.*, p. 89.

96. William Ashurst was a friend of Garrison and a contributor to the *Liberator*. For Ashurst *see* Holyoake, *Sixty Years*, pp. 182-86; *Dictionary of National Biography*.

97. *History of Woman Suffrage*, III, 838 n., 841; Blackburn, *op. cit.*, pp. 63-64; J. L. and B. Hammond, *James Stansfeld, A Victorian Champion of Sex Equality*, pp. 286-87; M. J. Shaen, *William Shaen: A Brief Sketch* (London, 1912); *see also ibid.*, *Memorials of Two Sisters*, p. 79. Ashurst, Stansfeld and Shaen were all members of the National Charter Association in 1841; Lovett, *op. cit.*, p. 259.

98. Elizabeth Cady Stanton to her cousin Elizabeth Smith Miller, the originator of the Bloomer costume, Sept. 20, 1855; Stanton and Blatch, *op. cit.*, II, 61.

99. Stanton and Blatch, *op. cit.*, I, 149; *History of Woman Suffrage*, I, 219 ff; Blackburn, *op. cit.*, p. 20. Harriet Taylor had become Mrs. John Stuart Mill the year before.

100. Stanton and Blatch, *op. cit.*, Vol. I, Chap. 15.

101. Hester Burton, *Barbara Bodichon* (London, 1949), p. 39.

102. It is interesting to note that W. H. Channing subsequently lived a good deal in England and his son became Member of Parliament for Kettering.

103. For the Blackwell family *see especially* Elizabeth Blackwell, *Pioneer Work in Opening the Medical Profession to Women* (London, 1895); Alice Stone Blackwell, *Lucy Stone* (Boston, 1930); *Dictionary of National Biography* and *Dictionary of American Biography*. Emily Blackwell graduated from the Cleveland Medical College to the study of surgery under Sir James Simpson in Edinburgh.

104. Joseph Parkes was also a friend and correspondent of Charles Sumner. *See* Sumner Papers, Widener Library, Harvard University.

Chapter 5

1. Although figures are scanty, it is possible that actual illiteracy may have been exaggerated. Perhaps as many as two-thirds of the population may have been able to read in the early years of the century, though the proportion able to write may have been much less. *See* R. J. Webb, *The British Working Class Reader, 1790–1848* (London, 1955), pp. 13-14, 21-23.

2. W. H. G. Armytage, "Some Aspects of American Influence on British Education," Address delivered to the Education Section of the British Association, August 21, 1956.

3. Joseph Dorfman, *The Economic Mind in American Civilization* (New York, 1946), II, 697.

4. There were even closer connections between Scottish and American universities, especially in the case of Edinburgh and Princeton, which continued virtually without interruption from the colonial period. The author regrets that it has not proved possible within the framework of this essay to deal adequately with Scottish education which, with its ideal of the public school and its equivalent of "the little red school house," was more democratic than the English, and closer to the American tradition.

5. It is interesting to note that the example of the adult school, established in Bristol in 1812, led to the founding in the following year of adult schools, largely for coloured people, in New York and Philadelphia; J. W. Hudson, *The History of Adult Education* (London, 1851), p. 6.

6. *Ibid.*, pp. 42-43, 49-51; J. W. Adamson, *English Education, 1789–1902* (Cambridge, 1930), pp. 37-39.

7. Hudson, *op. cit.*, p. 45; Carl Bode, *The American Lyceum* (New York, 1956), p. 240.

8. Hudson, *op. cit.*, p. 217.

9. Bode, *op. cit.*, p. 10.

10. Claxton, who returned to Britain in 1836, was the self-educated mechanic,

characteristic of the times. He manufactured scientific apparatus for lyceums and schools. *See* Timothy Claxton, *Memoir of a Mechanic* (Boston, 1839); and his *Hints to Mechanics on Self-Education and Mutual Instruction* (London, 1839), Chap. 1; Hudson, *op. cit.*, pp. 38-39; Bode, *op. cit.*, pp. 120-22; M. T. Hodgen, *Workers' Education in England and the United States* (London, 1925), p. 46 n. *The American Journal of Education,* 1826–1831, is an excellent source.

11. It is worth noting in passing that the bequest of $500,000 to the United States by the Englishman, James Smithson, was to be for the "growth and diffusion of knowledge." After years of debate in Congress this bequest materialized in 1846 as the Smithsonian Institute in Washington, a combination of popular museum of science, art gallery and library. Its foundation and its emphasis on popular science was largely due to the efforts of Robert Dale Owen, by that time a Congressman from Indiana.

12. *See* Bode, *op. cit.*, Chap. 1.

13. Hudson, *op. cit.*, p. vi.

14. *Ibid.*, p. 12.

15. Henry Brougham, "Practical Observations on the Education of the People," *Edinburgh Review,* Vol. XLI (1824); Hodgen, *op. cit.*, pp. 41-42.

16. A. E. Dobbs, *Education and Social Movements 1700–1850* (London, 1919), pp. 224-25.

17. *See* Hodgen, *op. cit.*, p. ix, and *passim.*

18. Black had arrived in England in 1834 with a plan for an educational association for working men, which influenced William Lovett in founding the London Working Men's Association. He also helped raise funds to pay Chartist fines. Lovett, *op. cit.*, p. 91; Hodgen, *op. cit.*, p. 87 n.; Dobbs, *op. cit.*, p. 227 n.

19. Holyoake, *op. cit.*, p. 292.

20. E. P. Cubberley: *Public Education in the United States* (rev. ed., Cambridge, Mass., 1934), pp. 137-41.

21. Memoir of Lancaster in *American Journal of Education,* June, 1861, pp. 355-62.

22. *See* John Griscom, *A Year in Europe* (New York, 1823), which is a little known, but useful account, reprinted in E. W. Knight (ed.), *Reports on European Education by John Griscom, Victor Cousin and Calvin Stowe* (New York, 1930); for Griscom and the Owens *see* J. W. Hiatt (ed.), "Diary of William Owen, 1824–25," Indiana Historical Society *Publications,* Vol. IV; Caroline D. Snedeker (ed.), "The Diaries of Donald Macdonald 1824–26," Indiana Historical Society *Publications,* Vol. XIV; *see also* Cubberley, *op. cit.*, pp. 354-55.

23. For Lancaster *see American Journal of Education,* June 1861, pp. 355-62; Joseph Lancaster, *The Lancasterian System of Education with Improvements, by Its Founder Joseph Lancaster of the Lancasterian Institute, Baltimore* (1821); William Russell, *Manual of Mutual Instruction* (Boston, 1826); the Joseph Lancaster Papers, Gratz Collection, Pennsylvania Historical Society, contain a voluminous correspondence on education.

24. Horace Mann, *Report of an Educational Tour* (2nd edition, 1843), pp. 43-44.

25. Cubberley, *op. cit.*, pp. 221-22.

26. Horace Mann, *op. cit.;* Cubberley, *op. cit.,* p. 362.

27. Calvin Stowe, *Report on Elementary Public Instruction in Europe* (1837); Victor Cousin, *Report on the State of Public Instruction in Prussia* (1836).

28. Adamson, *op. cit.,* p. 142.

29. It is noteworthy that Forster, a cousin of the Gurneys, was a leader in Parliament of the Unionist sympathizers during the American Civil War.

30. Armytage, *op. cit.,* p. 303.

31. Charles Gibbon, *The Life of George Combe* (London, 1878), I, 163, 205-07, 289-93.

32. *Ibid.,* II, 44.

33. *Loc. cit.*

34. Letter to Sir James Clark, *ibid.,* II, 76.

35. Combe's writings were based upon Horace Mann's reports. *Ibid.,* II, 128, 237.

36. *Ibid.,* II, 292.

37. S. E. Maltby, *Manchester and the Movement for National Elementary Education* (Manchester, 1918), p. 68 and n.; Margaret (Bright) Lucas was the temperance and feminist leader referred to above, p. 122.

38. Gibbon, *op. cit.,* II, 318.

39. Elizabeth Hoon Cawley (ed.), *The American Diaries of Richard Cobden* (Princeton, 1952), p. 121.

40. Richard Cobden, *England, Ireland and America* (Edinburgh, 1836), p. 33 n.

41. *See* Armytage, *op. cit.,* p. 302.

42. Cobden to W. Tait, Aug. 17, 1838; John Morley, *The Life of Richard Cobden* (London, 1881), I, 127.

43. Cobden to Geo. Combe, July 14, 1846; *ibid.,* I, 410.

44. Cobden to Geo. Combe, May 15, 1848; *ibid.,* II, 21-22.

45. John Bright and J. E. Thorold Rogers (eds.), *Cobden's Speeches on Questions of Public Policy* (London, 1903), p. 596, quoted in Armytage, *op. cit.,* p. 302.

46. Bright and Rogers, *op. cit.,* p. 609.

47. *Ibid.,* p. 600.

48. Cobden to Combe, April 24, 1848; Morley, *op. cit.,* II, 21.

49. Cobden to Combe, November 9, 1850; *ibid.,* II, 84.

50. Maltby, *op. cit.,* p. 89.

51. The American example was implemented by powerful addresses to meetings of the L. P. S. A. and N. P. S. A. by visiting Americans; Maltby, *op. cit.,* p. 81 n.

Chapter 6

1. Abdy, *op. cit.,* III, 311.

2. *The Beacon,* June 9, 1838.

3. *Working Man's Advocate,* July 6, 1844; J. G. Rayback, "The American

Working Man and the Anti-Slavery Crusade," *Journal of Economic History,* Vol. III (1943); F. J. Klingberg, "Harriet Beecher Stowe and Social Reform in England," *loc. cit.*; George Shepperson, "Harriet Beecher Stowe and Scotland," *Scottish Historical Review,* Vol. XXXII (1953). Mr. Shepperson calls attention both to the conscientiousness of Mrs. Stowe's inquiries into the conditions of the working class and to the prejudice against her in Scotland created by her friendship with the Duchess of Sutherland, which linked her name with the miseries caused by evictions from the Sutherland estates.

4. R. Harrison, "British Labour and the Confederacy: A Note on the Southern Sympathies of some British working class journals and leaders during the American Civil War," *International Review of Social History,* Vol. II (1957).

5. *Birney Letters,* I, 558.

6. Cobden to Livesey, Oct. 10, 1849; Morley, *op. cit.,* II, 59.

7. Cobden to Ashworth, Dec. 13, 1849, *ibid.,* II. 61; the letter also refers, significantly, to an American example: "The Americans have a clearer perception of the evils of drunkenness upon the political and material prospects of the people, and their leading men set an example of temperance on all public occasions. I lately read an account of a great political meeting in New Hampshire at which Daniel Webster presided, when fifteen hundred persons sat down to a dinner at which not a drop of wine, spirits or beer was drunk. Depend on it, they were more than a match for four times their numbers of wine-bibbers."

8. Cobden to Ashworth, April 18, 1842; Morley, *op. cit.,* I, 230-31.

9. Cobden to Combe, July 14, 1846; *ibid.,* I, 411.

10. Hobhouse, *op. cit.,* p. 57; Richard, *op. cit.,* pp. 267-68; Prentice, *op. cit.,* I, 276; G. D. H. Cole, "Joseph Sturge" in *Chartist Portraits* (London, 1941), pp. 172-73.

11. Lovett, *op. cit.,* pp. 36, 56-57, 273, 321-22.

12. Klingberg, "Harriet Beecher Stowe and Social Reform in England," *loc. cit.*

13. Letter to Frederick Cobden, Oct. 5, 1838; Morley, *op. cit.,* I, 126.

14. *Baltimore Gazette,* quoted in *Niles' Register,* Sept. 6, 1828; T. P. Martin, "Cotton and Wheat in Anglo-American Trade and Politics, 1846-52," *Journal of Southern History,* Vol. I (1934).

15. *Manchester Guardian,* June 2, 1821, quoted in T. P. Martin, "Conflicting Cotton Interests at Home and Abroad, 1848-57," *Journal of Southern History,* Vol. VII (1941).

16. For this paragraph *see especially* the following important articles by T. P. Martin, "Some International Aspects of the Anti-Slavery Movement, 1818-1823," *Journal of Economic and Business History,* Vol. I, 1928-29; "The Upper Mississippi Valley in Anglo-American Anti-Slavery and Free Trade Relations, 1837-42," *Mississippi Valley Historical Review,* Vol. XV (1928); "Cotton and Wheat in Anglo-American Trade and Politics, 1846-52," *Journal of Southern History,* Vol. I (1934); "Conflicting Cotton Interests at Home and Abroad, 1848-57," *Journal of Southern History,* Vol. VII

(1941); "Free Trade and the Oregon Question, 1842–46," in *Facts and Factors in Economic History*, by students of E. F. Gay (Cambridge, Mass., 1932).

17. Harriet Martineau, *Society in America*, I, 307.

18. *Nineteenth Annual Report* of the Manchester Chamber of Commerce (Manchester, 1840); quoted in T. P. Martin, *The Upper Mississippi Valley in Anglo-American Anti-Slavery and Free Trade Relations*.

19. A. Prentice, *A Tour in the United States, with Two Lectures on Emigration* (Manchester, 1849), pp. 12-13; *see also* pp. 46, 48-49.

20. T. E. Drake, *op. cit.*, p. 115; N. B. Wilkinson, "The Philadelphia Free Produce Attack upon Slavery," *Pennsylvania Magazine of History*, Vol. 66 (1942).

21. Klingberg, *The Anti-Slavery Movement*, p. 192.

22. Prentice, *History of the Anti-Corn Law League*, I, 231-32; Stoddart, *op. cit.*, p. 124; English, *op. cit.*, pp. 378-80; the agreement included a recognition by the League of a responsibility to support the British India Society in its aims once the Corn Laws had been repealed, an undertaking which John Bright later made efforts to honor.

23. G. D. H. Cole, *op. cit.*, pp. 181-82; Hobhouse, *op. cit.*, p. 69; Richard, *op. cit.*, Chap. 13.

24. Speech to the Council of the League, Manchester, September, 1842; Morley, *op. cit.*, I, 249.

25. Harriet Martineau to Maria Chapman, March 15, 1845, *Autobiography*, III, 245-46.

26. Letter to George Thompson, 1839; Phillips, *Published Addresses*, pp. 8-11.

27. Quoted in Sturge, *A Visit to the United States*, pp. 156-58.

28. Joshua Leavitt, *Memorial to Congress on the Wheat Interests of the Northwestern States*, 1841; *see also* Birney *Letters*, I, 580-81, 594; Sturge, *op. cit.*, pp. 110, 148-58; Prentice, *op. cit.*, I, 241, 263; *Emancipator*, December 24, 1840.

29. F. Merk, "The British Corn Crisis of 1845–46 and the Oregon Treaty," *Agricultural History*, Vol. VIII (1934). C. R. Fay, *The Corn Laws and Social England* (Cambridge, 1932), pp. 116-20.

30. P. W. Bidwell, "The New England Emigrant Aid Company and English Cotton Supply Associations," *American Historical Review*, Vol. XXIII (1917).

31. For other aspects of the wheat versus cotton controversy in its relation to the Civil War *see especially* Bernard Schmidt, "The Influence of Wheat and Cotton in Anglo-American Relations during the Civil War," *Iowa Journal of History and Politics*, Vol. XVI (1918); J. P. Bretz, "The Economic Background of the Liberty Party," *American Historical Review*, Vol. XXXIV (1929); M. P. Claussen, "Peace Factors in Anglo-American Relations," *Mississippi Valley Historical Review*, Vol. XXVI (1939–40).

32. Prentice, *op. cit.*, I, 1-2.

33. Richard Cobden, *England, Ireland and America* (Edinburgh edition, 1836).

34. *Ibid.*, p. 11.

35. It must be noted, however, that Cobden made India the great exception to a liberal colonial policy.
36. *Ibid.*, p. 12.
37. *Loc. cit.*
38. *Ibid.*, pp. 6-7, 25-26.
39. *Ibid.*, p. 6.
40. *Ibid.*, p. 25.
41. *Ibid.*, p. 31.
42. Morley, *op. cit.*, II, 483.
43. Cobden, *op. cit.*, p. 11.
44. Cobden to Henry Ashworth, Feb. 7, 1862; Morley, *op. cit.*, II, 396.
45. Morley, *op. cit.*, II, 483.
46. *Ibid.*, I, 186.
47. H. B. Stanton, *Reforms and Reformers* (New York, 1849), pp. iv-v.
48. Cobden, *op. cit.*, p. 34.
49. For a perceptive analysis of these later relations *see* H. M. Pelling, *America and the British Left: From Bright to Bevan* (London, 1956), *passim.* *See also* Frank Thistlethwaite: "America and Two Nations of Englishmen," *Virginia Quarterly Review*, Vol. 31 (1955); "The Citadel and the Caravan: Anglo-American Relations in the Twentieth Century," *American Quarterly*, Vol. IX (1957); "What Is Un-American?", *Cambridge Journal*, Vol. V (1952) *The Great Experiment, An Introduction to the History of the American People* (Cambridge, 1955), Chap. 12.

Index

harper ✦ torchbooks

HUMANITIES AND SOCIAL SCIENCES

American Studies

Anthropology & Sociology

Art and Art History

*The New American Nation Series, edited by Henry Steele Commager and Richard B. Morris.

†*The Rise of Modern Europe Series*, edited by William L. Langer.

5

NATURAL SCIENCES AND MATHEMATICS

Biological Sciences

Chemistry

Geography

History of Science

Mathematics

Code to Torchbook Libraries:

TB/1+	: The Cloister Library
TB/501+	: The Science Library
TB/1001+	: The Academy Library
TB/2001+	: The Bollingen Library
TB/3001+	: The University Library

A LETTER TO THE READER

Overseas, there is considerable belief that we are a country of extreme conservatism and that we cannot accommodate to social change.

Books about America in the hands of readers abroad can help change those ideas.

The U. S. Information Agency cannot, by itself, meet the vast need for books about the United States.

You can help.

Harper Torchbooks provides three packets of books on American history, economics, sociology, literature and politics to help meet the need.

To send a packet of Torchbooks (retailing at $10.85 to $12.00) overseas, all you need do is send your check for $7 (which includes cost of shipping) to Harper & Row. The U. S. Information Agency will distribute the books to libraries, schools, and other centers all over the world.

I ask every American to support this program, part of a worldwide BOOKS USA campaign.

I ask you to share in the opportunity to help tell others about America.

EDWARD R. MURROW
Director,
U. S. Information Agency

PACKET I: Twentieth Century America

Dulles/America's Rise to World Power, 1898-1954
Cochran/The American Business System, 1900-1955
Zabel, Editor/Literary Opinion in America (two volumes)
Drucker/The New Society: *The Anatomy of Industrial Order*
Fortune Editors/America in the Sixties: *The Economy and the Society*

PACKET II: American History

Billington/The Far Western Frontier, 1830-1860
Mowry/The Era of Theodore Roosevelt and the
  Birth of Modern America, 1900-1912
Faulkner/Politics, Reform, and Expansion, 1890-1900
Cochran & Miller/The Age of Enterprise: *A Social History of*
  Industrial America
Tyler/Freedom's Ferment: *American Social History from the*
  Revolution to the Civil War

PACKET III: American History

Hansen/The Atlantic Migration, 1607-1860
Degler/Out of Our Past: *The Forces that Shaped Modern America*
Probst, Editor/The Happy Republic: *A Reader in Tocqueville's America*
Alden/The American Revolution, 1775-1783
Wright/The Cultural Life of the American Colonies, 1607-1763

Your gift will be acknowledged directly to you by the overseas recipient.
Simply fill out the coupon, detach and mail with your check or money order.

HARPER & ROW, PUBLISHERS · BOOKS USA DEPT.
49 East 33rd Street, New York 16, N. Y.

Packet I ☐   Packet II ☐   Packet III ☐

Please send the BOOKS USA library packet(s) indicated above, in my
name, to the area checked below. Enclosed is my remittance in the
amount of _____ for _____ packet(s) at $7.00 each.

_____ Africa   _____ Latin America

_____ Far East   _____ Near East

Name_____

Address_____

_____

NOTE: *This offer expires December 31, 1966.*